THE
ADULLAM
EXPERIENCE

WHERE BROKEN MEN
BECOME THE MIGHTY

"Stephen Miller is a mighty man. I have known Stephen for more than 30 years and can promise you that he is not just a world-record-setting Strong Man physically, but he is also strong spiritually, emotionally, mentally, and relationally. I highly recommend Stephen and whatever he is inspired to say and write—especially to men. Without question, you will find great strength in *The Adullam Experience*."

—**TERRY A SMITH**, Lead Pastor of The Life Christian Church, West Orange, New Jersey
Author of *The Hospitable Leader*

"The English bishop, Stephen Gardiner, once stated, 'The frame of the cave leads to the frame of man.' In light of that, may I suggest that, if we must have a cave experience, and if that cave is going to frame us, it is paramount that we choose the right cave! Stephen Miller has identified the perfect cavern that housed an imperfect man and his band of imperfect friends who went on to do heroic and world-changing feats. He brings out timeless truths that will help frame a man into the person God always intended for him to be. You're holding in your hands a ticket to the Cave of Adullam, and then on beyond your wildest dreams."

—**SCOTT R. JONES**, Sr. Pastor, Grace Church, Humble, Texas

"All of life is lived on levels and arrived at in stages. My friend Stephen Miller shares great truths he learned from his own Adullam. Whatever stage or level you are currently on, you can benefit from these truths."

—**G.F. WATKINS**, Founder of Powerhouse Church, Katy, Texas / Jordan Ranch

"For a message to resonate deeply with a reader, it must come from a place rooted firmly in the personal experience of the author. *The Adullam Experience* is such a book. Stephen speaks with authority about the principles necessary to build character in the hearts of men because he has devoted his life to doing so for many years with great effectiveness."

    — DR. RICHARD HEARD, Sr. Pastor, Inspire Church, Houston, Texas

THE
ADULLAM
EXPERIENCE

WHERE BROKEN MEN
BECOME THE MIGHTY

STEPHEN MILLER

HIGH BRIDGE BOOKS
HOUSTON

Special Thanks

A special thanks to my wife, Mary. Thank you for these many years together. Life has shown us just about everything it can. Highs and lows, good times and trying times, but we're still here. Your strength and determination are amazing. I am grateful for the mother and nana you have been to our tribe. Thank you for believing in me. You have made so much possible for all of us. May God give you great health and joy for many years to come.

To my amazing children, Stephanie and Josh Bowers, Bethanie Miller, and Stephen Miller II: you are all the best. My greatest desire is to leave the legacy that all of you deserve—at least, I will live my whole life trying.

To my incredible grandchildren, Jaxon, Kensington, and Dylan: my daily prayer is to pass something greater to you than what I've received. I often say, "The legacy a man wants to leave is the legacy he must live." With God's grace, strength, and wisdom, that is the sum total of the pursuit of my life.

To my parents, Jim Miller and Bobbie Bafford: while doing it separately, you both managed to model many valuable traits and dynamics. I love you both for your individual strengths and qualities. You have truly contributed to a legacy that will outlast both of you.

To my pastor and mentor, Dr. Richard Heard: thank you for the model you've provided for men who long to "dwell in the secret place." So much of what I speak, live, and write about has come from your influence and the time we've spent together in the cave.

And, most importantly, to my Heavenly Father: You keep giving me things I don't deserve and protecting me from things I do deserve. You have promised to be a "Father to the fatherless," and *that*, among so many other things, You have certainly been. You are my life, my breath, my salvation and healing, and my being.

Contents

1

Introduction to Adullam

David left Gath and escaped to the cave of Adullam. When his brothers and his father's household heard about it, they went down to him there. All those who were in distress or in debt or discontented gathered around him, and he became their commander. About four hundred men were with him.

—1 Samuel 22:1-3 NIV

This is perhaps my favorite story in scripture— the reasons are many. I too have been in debt and broken. I've been in distress and had seasons of unspeakable disappointment. More than once, I have faced burnout. I've trained alone for goals that no one thought I could ever attain. And the list can go on.

Perhaps my experience has not been as severe as some, but I've endured enough pain, failure, and set-back to really appreciate this metamorphosis. There's nothing like the process that shows us broken, wounded, and hurting men rising from their plight to become more than they ever dreamed they could be.

Many stories of radical transformation have occurred in some of the most unusual and unexpected places. Joseph—while in prison. The children of Israel—while laboring as captives in the brickyards of Egypt. Daniel—in the lions' den. Jonah—in the belly of a great whale. Paul—clinging to driftwood after his ship sank. John the Baptist—in the wilderness, living on locusts and wild honey. And the Apostle John—banished to a deserted island after an unsuccessful execution attempt, where he received the unparalleled "Revelation of Jesus Christ."

But this cave … it was something profoundly special!

The enemies of David had chased him into the cave and meant to *hurt* him. Instead, God used the cave to *herd* him. To give him an opportunity to pull himself together and restore him. Then God brought 400 more potentially great men as well as his family to transform them together.

Think of it—broken, disillusioned, burnt-out men, running from the law—came together in a desolate cave, only to emerge as a group of the most fierce, battle-ready, heroic warriors the world has ever known! Going into the cave, they're described as a pretty pitiful group of guys on the run. But when they emerged from this cave, they are forever referred to as *"David's Mighty Men."*

The historical account of King David and these men is one of the greatest stories of total transformation in history. And I believe your story will be similar!

You mimic being a great man, and before you know it, you have become one!

Perhaps you have already concluded that you're not broken, in debt, or disheartened. I certainly don't want to over-incriminate every living man, but the truth is we are all broken. We are living in a fallen world where real masculinity is under a myriad of subtle attacks. Our culture— heck, our world—wants to diminish the very idea of true masculinity, and there are reasons why!

I want you to intensely digest the content I'm going to share with you, then take action. I believe that most people have been educated far beyond their level of obedience—or they know a lot more than what they have done.

At some point, you will have to put down the remote control, toss the bag of potato chips and can of soda, step up, and take some action. Taking action to become a mighty man is imperative. Your family is waiting on you; your church is waiting for you; your community is waiting for you; your friends are waiting on you, but most importantly, God is waiting on you!

Most people are educated
far beyond their level of obedience.

That's the best part: God is waiting on you. He knows exactly what you're capable of being. Having created you in His own image of greatness, He is ready, willing, and able to equip, empower, and elevate you to be a Mighty Man!

While we don't know everything that contributed to the radical metamorphosis of these men, we do know that the collective transformation that occurred is nothing short of a phenomenon. Their condition when they arrived has been shared with us. It is summarized with these three conditions: *distressed, in debt,* and *discontented.* Those may be somewhat broad terms, but in this present day, they would look something like this.

Distressed (Scarcity)

Never having enough. Modern men constantly feel the impact of scarcity. Quite different from poverty, even after you have acquired plenty of money, toys, and hobbies, it still seems there is never enough with scarcity:

- Never enough cash
- Never enough time
- Never enough adventure
- Never enough space
- Never enough sex
- Never enough respect
- Never enough honor
- Never enough energy
- Never enough influence

And the list goes on and on.

Most people are deeply rooted in the Scarcity Mentality. They see life as having only so much, as if there was only one pie out there. And if someone should get a bigger piece of the pie, it would mean less for everyone else.
—Stephen Covey

The demon of *scarcity* is a brutal spirit that can be traced all the way back to Lucifer himself. He had everything — position, prestige, power, presence, and priority (perhaps the highest-ranking archangel in heaven), yet it wasn't enough. Scarcity makes you focus on what you *don't* have rather than what you *do* have. When you're not properly aligned with God, there's never enough of anything. But when you're walking with God, whose name itself implies that He is "more than enough," scarcity begins to diminish. Unfortunately, scarcity is a familiar attitude of way too many men today.

In Debt

Far beyond financial hardship, many men are feeling exhausted from giving, giving, and giving with so few returning the favor. They live in a constant state of deficit, always giving much more than they are receiving. You were not created to remain in a constant state of depletion. At some point, you will collapse or implode. The Hebrew word used here actually implies that these men were fugitives of the law, running away from their debts. That's what this kind of debt makes you want to do: run!

Discontented

Emotions, demands, the expectations of others, and pressure from every side can leave the average man with a general sense of unfulfillment. Sometimes this feeling is so overwhelming that men are almost willing to sit and watch what little they do have burn to the ground. Consequently, most men keep trying to present some semblance of "got-it-togetherness," living their lives for the most part in a sedated state—sedated by all the wrong things, unfortunately. But you can't escape the emptiness of dissatisfaction. Even though it may seem easier to just live in an induced state of numbness, trust me—at some point, it will come crashing down upon you. *It's the nature of the beast.*

Inaction breeds doubt and fear. Action breeds confidence and courage. If you want to conquer fear, do not sit at home and think about it. Go out and get busy!
—Dale Carnegie

Somewhere early on, David's men had to come to the realization: "I have been lied to! I was handed a life-script that was fatally flawed."

Something very significant had to change. Men like this never do great exploits. They try to survive as long as possible and, at best, prevent a complete explosion or implosion of their life.

Great exploits are performed by healed men. *Complete* men. After the cave experience, the endless exploits of David's men have been etched into the history of humanity.

So how did it happen? To what training regimen were these men subjected? What kind of program did David present to them? Scripture is silent. But you need look no further than David himself and his own experience in the cave.

Remember this: You don't produce what you want, wish, or hope for. You reproduce what you *are*!

David's own progressive restoration was the model for transforming 400 broken, defeated men into mighty, healed, free, and focused men!

My mission in life is to facilitate as many Adullam experiences for as many men as I possibly can. I trust this book will initiate such an experience for you. What is the goal? What does it look like? What are the characteristics of a man who is mighty?

- He is an authentic follower of Jesus.
- He is always increasing his cognitive capacity.
- He has great control over his emotions.
- He loves his queen and leads his home and his tribe.
- He takes care of his temple and becomes the healthiest version of himself.
- He is dependable—his word is his bond.
- He's the guy everyone in his world wants to emulate.
- He gets paid what he's worth, not what he's settled for.
- He lives an elevated life. Right-standing, peace, and joy define his life.

Along with hundreds of others, I beckon you to come into the Cave of Adullam and take this journey so that you will emerge as the mighty man you were created to be.

He who conquers others is strong;
He who conquers himself is mighty!
—Lao Tzu

Small-Group Discussion Points

- The three conditions mentioned in 1 Samuel 22:1-3 were: *Distress, in Debt,* and *Discontentment.* How have you experienced any of these conditions in your own life?
- How have you addressed these conditions?
- What steps have you taken to avoid falling back into them?

2

The Plot

What happened? How did we get here? Who or what broke us? When did it even happen? Why and how did it happen? These are but a few of the questions in the minds of men today. Let's explore.

For King David, the plot was complex, as it is with many men.

1. On one hand, he was trying to do what God had called him to do and what the prophet Samuel had anointed him to do: become God's next man to rule over Israel. Until now, he had been on a roll—popular, successful, and celebrated all over Israel. But now, everything had changed. No longer were his enemies impressed or afraid of him. His popularity had waned. What had worked before no longer worked. He had dedicated so much of his time and focus to becoming king that it seems he had become oblivious to the fact that God still needed to transform him into the man who could handle that responsibility. In other words, David

had gotten consumed with the call instead of the man who was answering the call.

2. Early success and popularity had pulled him away from fully seeking after God. Now, he was under attack on every side by an enemy he didn't know how to defeat. Not so long ago, he had taken out a giant named Goliath with nothing more than a slingshot and a few smooth stones. But now, nothing was working. Adding to his woes, he was feeling shunned by his family, betrayed by his friends, mocked by his wife, and perplexed by the jealousy and envy of his mentor. Issues from his childhood that he thought had been forever settled were now surfacing to sabotage his success.

And as the "law of association" would have it, 400 men in the region who were feeling broken, beaten, and discouraged and who were running for their lives had begun to search for David. When they found him in the cave, they readily came to join him.

I've intentionally left a gap between the time of David's arrival in Adullam and when the others arrived. That's the time that defines the Adullam Experience—what occurred with and to David first becomes the model for broken men becoming the mighty.

While these men weren't exactly the guys you would choose to build an army, David welcomed them. He was thrilled for them to come because he knew that amazing things happen in the cave! They had already happened to him.

Now, let's compare David's two-fold dilemma with the reality of our present day.

The Injustice

In Isaiah 3:1, God's judgment upon Judah and Israel for their rebellion was to remove the warriors and mighty men. In fact, He listed several things that would be removed, in this particular order:

- bread and water
- the warrior and the mighty man
- judges
- prophets and seers
- elders, honorable men, etc.

Have you noticed something here? By virtue of the order God listed these things in, He established what is most important to prevent the collapse of a society or civilization. Immediately after bread and water (the essentials for life) came the warriors and mighty men. When men fail to stand up and lead, everything in their world begins to collapse— as does the culture in which they live.

God's intent here was to bring Judah and Israel to their knees—not for destruction, but for correction, so they would repent. This Divine intuition illuminates for us a critical truth: next to the bare essentials of life, the most important way to keep a nation alive and prosperous is to produce warriors and mighty men.

To provoke them to repentance, God would temporarily remove the warriors and mighty men and then subsequently restore them. But the adversary's intention for removing the warriors and mighty men is for irréversible destruction.

A dark, unseen spiritual force is seeking to minimize or completely remove all evidence of masculine leadership. Of course, this dark force knows all too well what will happen when real men begin to lead.

When Pharaoh heard that a child was about to be born who would threaten his world of corruption and dictatorial rule, he panicked! He resolved to kill every newborn male in the land. Not one of these male children would be allowed to realize his destiny and purpose. Thankfully, God prevailed, and Moses was born. Eventually, he would lead an entire nation out of slavery and into their promised land.

Centuries later, King Herod experienced a very similar threat to his corrupt kingdom. A child would be born, specifically the Messiah and Savior of the world. Herod's resolve, like Pharaoh's, was to kill every newborn male child. But once again, God prevailed. Christ was born and would redeem and bring the entire human creation back to God.

We know that this kind of attempt at extinction would never fly in America. We are too strong and too civilized to tolerate such an edict from a tyrannical ruler. It would produce an uprising such as the world has never seen. However, the same thing *is* essentially happening right under our noses!

I believe that our adversary is very much aware of this reality and has perpetrated the most cynical and hideous strategy ever known. The masculine soul is being disintegrated and neutralized through trendy but diabolical influences. Shame and guilt are commonly associated with everything that appears to be masculine. Regardless of what millenniums of history should have taught us, masculinity has come to be considered toxic!

Throughout the ages, every distinguished civilization has been identified (and celebrated) by its great warrior class. These traditions have been heroically confirmed from one generation to the next through poetry and folk tales, as well as factual, historical writings.

Think about the Spartans, Roman legions, Vikings, Knights, Maasai Tribe, Samurai, Aztecs, and more. Each time we congratulate a strong warrior class, it always seems to have been promoted by a nation that either was or was at least becoming tremendously successful. When real men—not immature, angry, broken youths running around thumping their chests in a pseudo-machismo posture— have become healed and complete, they will assume their role in leadership. Subsequently, everything in their world will begin to prosper!

Although a warrior spirit may be alive and well in the mantras of our nation's fighting forces, as a society, we have begun to shun the very idea of a warrior. Strong masculinity has moved far down the social ladder. The general population of men is desperately missing the warrior class. While we would no longer show up on horses with spears, swords, and shields, we should at least demonstrate strong leadership in our families, communities, and nation. That's where real men need to show up.

Sadly, we live in a nation that almost abhors the idea of strong masculinity. From the gender-neutral movement's total assault on masculinity across the board, our culture is desperately trying to force our boys to become less masculine and more feminine.

We have gotten so far off track it's even okay to choose which gender you'd like to be, but it's not okay to identify as a warrior who will defend himself, his family, his ideals, and his country. And of course, when boys choose a gender for their life's existence, the heavier influence of our culture would prefer that they choose female.

Just check out what The American Enterprise Institute's acclaimed Christina Hoff Summers wrote in her book, *The War Against Boys: How Misguided Feminism Is Harming Our Young Men*:

> America's public schools are set up to obliterate all that is masculine and establish femininity as the human norm: The underlying slogan/agenda is 'men are the new women.' It has become fashionable to attribute pathology to millions of healthy male children.

Her book insightfully documents how our culture has turned against our boys. "We have forgotten the undeniable truth that the active energy, competitiveness, and adventurism of a normal, healthy boy is responsible for much of what is right in our world."

She goes on to say:

> No one denies that a boy's aggressive tendencies must be checked and channeled in constructive ways. Boys need discipline, respect, moral guidance, love, and tolerant understanding, but they do not need to be pathologized. This is a bad time to be a boy in America. Routinely regarded

as proto-sexist, potential harassers, and perpet-
uators of gender inequity, boys live under a
cloud of censure.

She even documents how the curriculums of our edu-
cational system are skewed toward girls' strengths rather
than boys'. As a case in point, she elaborates on why word
problems are emphasized in math and writing essays in science classes, among other examples.

We could go on and on about other popular trends,
such as the following:

- Leaving birth certificates blank under "sex"
  so a child can later decide for themselves
  how they wish to be identified (yes, this is really happening).
- Removing gender specific pronouns, such as
  "him" and "her" from public conversation.
  This is also happening right now in many
  public schools.
- Mocking and ridiculing masculinity as some
  kind of toxic dysfunction through entertain-
  ment and art. Seriously?!

Unfortunately, many males who are understandably
incensed and seeking to revolt against this craziness are not
moving any closer to a solution. Some of the unfortunate
reactions that we see are:

1. Overly sensitive guys who will do anything to avoid conflict, criticism, or inconvenience. Their main goal is just to please women. They'll say whatever they think they're supposed to say and do whatever they think is expected of them.

2. Indifferent, detached guys who only want to be left alone in their man caves to play video games and drink beer with their like-minded friends.

3. The super sophisticated, "educated" folks who think this dilemma can best be addressed with endless philosophical debates. These are the guys who try to "reasonably" explain everything away as the natural evolution of civilization. The smarter, higher-class people see this and just flow with it. They think putting lipstick on a pig means it will no longer be a pig.

4. Then we have the "over-performers." This behavioral dynamic prompts people to react whenever they feel a particular identity is under attack, especially if it correlates with their own identity. To respond by over-performing only perpetuates the problem rather than solving it. If your identity is flawed, over-performing will only give your adversary extra ammo against you.

5. We also see straight-up "thug mentality!" This includes guys who lack the ability to articulate the error of this injustice and cannot respond in a well-thought-out, strategic way.

Instead, their only concern is to prove their toughness and masculinity with insensitivity and anger. They may even bounce around to different causes since they provide an opportunity for them to vent their frustration and rage.

None of the above examples are correct, and none will exemplify the mindset and life of a true warrior.

There is a better way to address this dilemma. The first is with truth and love. A bad model cannot simply be replaced by another bad one. We need a time-tested, proven, and impeccable model. Today's man must look to Jesus Christ, the perfect model of masculinity and leadership. Women respectfully admired Him; children wanted to follow Him; other men wanted to imitate Him; the sick, wounded, and hurting were filled with hope by Him; the crowds were inspired by being around Him. But His enemies were intimidated by Him, and the self-righteous, religious people were exposed by Him. Yes, the world needed Him—and He knew it. And He was ready for them!

His life was an uncommon blend of absolute power and authority, as well as totally authentic humility. Yes, He was strong and resolute, but He also had feelings. He was power and authority personified (without trying to prove it). As the Son of God, He relished the idea of serving people. With a seemingly insurmountable task, He knew His time was short. But in just three and a half years, His mission was accomplished.

Humanity was forever changed as He shook the whole world! And, yes, He also had a cave. But perhaps that's another book (think what 30 years in a carpenter's shop could do!).

Marianne Williamson says,

> Our greatest fear is not that we are inadequate, but that we are powerful beyond measure. It is our light, not our darkness that frightens us. We ask ourselves, "Am I to be brilliant, gorgeous, handsome, talented and fabulous?" Actually, who are you not to be? You are a child of God. To play small does not serve the world. There is nothing enlightened about shrinking so that other people won't feel insecure around you. We were born to make manifest the glory of God within us. It is not just in some; it is in everyone. And, as we let our own light shine, we sub-consciously give others permission to do the same. As we are liberated from our fear, our presence automatically liberates others.

Is it possible that injustices and the devil's sinister, evil plot have exposed issues just beneath the surface of most men's lives? Things we have forgotten about or assumed that time would heal? Or a level of dysfunction that consistently sabotages our future?

In summary, broken, depressed, angry, and hurting men will never tackle a memorable exploit or change history in a positive way. But mighty men will! Those who joined David probably had no clue about their potential. But they were willing to commit their lives to an authentic leader. They trained, healed, and then emerged as the historical Mighty Men!

Now, it's your turn. It's your turn to work hard, confront your fears, lose your baggage, and become who God already knows you are. The challenge has been given. What will you do? Will you put this book down and return to your sedate life or become defensive about my direct approach? OR will you keep reading, continue with an "all in" attitude, and allow the complete man within you to emerge? I pray you will do the latter. You won't regret the journey. Come on. Let's get this done!

Small-Group Discussion Points

- *Don't allow shame, guilt, or regret to become part of your motivation.* Guilt has never been an effective motivator. Since you did not create this dilemma, you're not to blame. But you must take responsibility.
- *Don't get mad; get motivated.* Anger only pulls you into a knee-jerk reaction. This is not the time for that. To address the dilemma, you must have calculated, strategic thought processes. How can you change—not the whole world, but your own? Albert Einstein said, "No particular challenge can be solved at the same level of consciousness in which it was created."
- *See God in everything, not just the problems.* These problems have been going on for centuries. But if God is not worried, anxious, or feeling any defeat, the question to ask every

day is: "Am I moving closer to or farther away from the problem?" The closer you are to Him, the closer you are to the right answers.

- *Don't rush out to find some psychology book.* So many of their observations range from one extreme to the next. When no one agrees on the final authority, there's no movement toward "true north." The Bible is the only time-tested, final authority on all that pertains to life and humanity. So skip the current arguments and rely on the Word.

3

The Cave

What was so amazing about Adullam? Was there anything specifically unique about this cave? Did it have some magical presence from past centuries? Or perhaps the ghosts of previous warriors or some type of vortex into the supernatural?

Nearly every truth about the cave of Adullam is two-fold, each with applications that do not conflict or contradict the other. Let's explore.

Perhaps the reason we are not privy to everything that happened in the cave is, in part, what made it so impacting. What happened in the cave stayed in the cave! It became a safe place, a den of brotherhood. In this secret place, men could encounter God with other men who shared their same feelings of desperation.

I do believe there was a distinct and powerful atmosphere in Adullam, but perhaps for reasons other than what most would think. Is it possible that the mere presence of these men, however beat up and dysfunctional they may have been, ignited a sense of empowerment that almost immediately began to change things? Wherever men gather together, strength and hope fill the air. The cave became their perfect starting point.

From David's account, the analogy of the cave had two applications. The first, as we have mentioned, was a place where men could gather to experience transformation. However, when we examine what happened to David before the 400 others joined him, the cave was a secret place of repentance and devotion. *The place of hiding became the place of healing.* Adullam was the perfect secret place where men could find yet an even deeper secret place. Both are necessary when a man is seeking to be complete.

Long before the potential mighty men joined him, the cave had become David's hiding place from his enemies. Perhaps he was confronted with this realization: if he had continued to seek God while in the palace as he had sought Him in the obscurity of his father's field, he would not have needed a place to hide. But instead of being swallowed up with regret and self-loathing, his hiding place was transformed into a place of intense renewal. Listen to his prayer when he first arrived at Adullam:

> God, I'm crying out to you!
> I lift up my voice boldly to beg for your mercy.
> I spill out my heart to you and tell you all my
> troubles.
> For when I was desperate, overwhelmed, and
> about to give up,
> you were the only one there to help.
> You gave me a way of escape
> from the hidden traps of my enemies.
> I look to my left and right to see if there is any-
> one who will help,
> but there's no one who takes notice of me.

I have no hope of escape, and no one cares
    whether I live or die.
So I cried out to you, Lord, my only hiding
    place.
You're all I have, my only hope in this life,
my last chance for help.
Please listen to my heart's cry,
for I am low and in desperate need of you!
Rescue me from all those who persecute me,
for I am no match for them.
Bring me out of this dungeon so I can declare
    your praise!
And all your godly lovers will celebrate
all the wonderful things you have done for me!
(Ps. 142 TPT)

In the context of gathering with other men, the degree of transformation you experience will be determined by the other men you have chosen. Your cave experience can't just be a "cool boys' club" or a relevant place to chill with other guys. I contend that the reason these men experienced such a phenomenal metamorphosis was because of David's personal encounter with God before they arrived. He had already addressed some of his own family issues and had once again become clear about his purpose.

Inexplicably, hurting men will produce hurting men. Beware of gatherings that are limited to guys trying to "one-up" each other about who got the rawest deal. Or even worse, a place to cover your juvenile dysfunction.

We don't want to hide out with other guys to minimize our iniquities or to find someone who will sympathize with us. We need the seclusion of the cave so we can be transformed. We want to be held accountable, challenged, supported, encouraged, and celebrated so that we may *give up, heal up,* and *get up*!

The average man today encounters spiritual defeat, but not from a lack of studying the Bible or attending a church worship service. Of course, it's the Word that will change us, and that intimate time in the presence of God will profoundly affect us.

But many today are dying spiritually because of this one fact: *We are not doing life together!* And certainly not in an environment where we can fellowship without fear of being judged unfairly. This freedom from judgment is not to feel comfortable or at ease with your faults. Rather, the fruit of a good cave experience will be restoration, renewal, and an awakening to your purpose and destiny.

The cave was a safe place for these guys to "come clean." But their time in the cave would never have been beneficial unless God had already transformed their leader.

It was David's personal life experiences that equipped him to be empathetic, but it was his victories that empowered him to be effective.

If you want to spark growth and elevation in your life, at some point, you will have to find a cave and a handful of guys with whom you can do life! That's the way it works.

You can't leap over a man's primal need for community and think you can work it all out just between "you and God." There *will* be some transformational moments just between you and God, but you will still have to work it out by walking with other like-minded men.

James 5:16 (KJV) tells us: *"Confess your faults one to another, and pray for one another, that you may be healed."* But where can a man go to confess his faults in a way that would bring healing without marring his character and reputation? The Apostle James implies that there is a context in which this can be exercised: among trusted people and in a trusted environment.

James was right! If we do not confess our faults, we will not be healed, but few of us have ever found such a place. Many of our "confession" experiences have been negative. We took that first step, opened up, and became vulnerable, only for it to backfire on us. Did we enter the wrong cave?

This does not mean that to be healed we must divulge every one of our moral transgressions to another guy. The key word here is "faults." Scripture teaches that there is a difference between a transgression and a fault. It also assures us that Jesus has taken care of both.

"But he was wounded for our transgressions, he was bruised for our iniquities" (Is. 53:5 KJV). A wound is an external injury, while a bruise is beneath the skin. Jesus was wounded externally for our transgressions (the external, visible violations of God's moral law), but He was also bruised internally for those things beneath the surface of our lives that no one sees or knows about. Of course, we can ask for His strength to keep us from doing things we don't *want* to do. But most men suffer more from "cause-oriented" wounds, the fractures beneath the surface of our lives.

If I punched someone for no justifiable reason, that's a transgression. But the iniquity is the deep-rooted anger that stems from who knows where and causes me to do foolish things. Deep within us, there is a longing—a compulsion to dive a little deeper than just those outward moral violations. We must go beneath the surface of our lives to root out things that make us lean toward destructive behavior patterns. We are longing for a place where broken men can *bear each other's burdens, pray for one another, and be healed*! That is the advantage of the cave.

In the cave, we become the authentic version of ourselves. Authenticity is not akin to perfection. It just means being an "original"—not copied or fake. Authentic men feel no compulsion to project something that is not real. They can live with flaws, but not secrets. It's called being perfectly imperfect.

You see, battling the secret things in your life is not the biggest problem. Regardless of your issues—whether it's an inferiority complex, insecurity, self-control, porn addiction, or anger—it's not the severity of the secret that will mess you up as much as the mere idea of having a secret.

Those internal contradictions have a way of establishing a dangerous and destructive pattern. We were not created to live and achieve our very best while always "looking over our shoulder." The longer you live a lie, the more broken you become. Your life becomes more and more fractured and less and less complete. Completeness is not the same as flawless. It just means that everything is pointing in the same direction. Every man needs an Adullam experience that will free him so he can heal up and get back on top where he belongs.

"It's not good for the man to be alone" (Gen. 2:18 NIV). Typically, we associate this exhortation from God in the context of marital intimacy. And that is true. But it goes far

beyond that application. The fact is, it's not good for a man to be alone *period*! Isolation is a battlefield on which we have not been anointed or equipped to win. God created us to be communal beings. To be our best, we must exist in a community. The best communities of men are found in caves!

You must find yourself a cave, but not just any cave. Not a cave that will minimize your dysfunctions, coddle your feelings, or stroke your ego. This cave must have a leader who can hear you while helping you. He must be able to challenge and hold you accountable while supporting you. He must have personally experienced distress, defeat, and brokenness, but also be well acquainted with transformation and the taste of victory. If he's not quite there yet, keep looking. There's another cave for you.

When you find it, there will always be a cave within the cave. Like David, his hiding place became a place of renewal and restoration. It won't just be a place to escape to and hang out with relevant men and be yourself. No, it will lead you to your own sacred place of repentance, rededication, devotion, and worship. This is the ultimate thrill of *"dwelling in the secret place of the Most-High God."* If your cave experience moves you toward your own secret place, then you have found the right cave. This is the brotherhood you have been looking for!

Small-Group Discussion Guide

- *Find a group of men where you can ease your way into fellowship.* You were meant to enjoy life in the context of community. If you can hang out with godly men who have the same common interests, that's even better!
- *Find good, godly mentors with whom you can connect.* If they are already in your life, learn to lean into them a little more. Share with them what you hope will be the outcome of your journey. Be slow to speak and quick to make thorough observations. Every man needs a mentor in his life.
- *Carve out a time for sacred devotion where you can discover your own secret place with God.* A cave within a cave is what you're really looking for. Secluded with other guys but absent from God is just another juvenile boys' club.

4

God Is First or You're Finished!

The most common complaint I hear from women and children concerning the men in their lives is this: "They won't stand up and take the lead." They want Dad to be more sensitive but not passive. They want him to lead but not drive. They want their husband/father to be a man of God. And I'm convinced that in their hearts, that's the kind of husband/father most men really want to be themselves. I've had this conversation with hundreds of men over the years about stepping up their leadership. My conclusion is that the main reason men won't lead—or can't lead—is because they themselves are not being led!

It is critical to note that before David could hide in Adullam and emerge victorious, he had to have a fresh encounter with God. It's possible that the God who had always been first in David's life as a boy was no longer his top priority. After all, in his youth, David had defeated a giant, delivered Israel from their enemies, married the king's daughter, and was well on his way to ruling the kingdom. His popularity had grown, songs were being written and sung about him, and his enemies feared him. *Maybe he had forgotten why!*

As everything started to unravel and he found himself in serious trouble, he began to think as many men do: "I've got this!" Well, at one time, he may have, but now it seems that he had lost it. Or at the very least, he had reached a point where he needed much more than what he had.

David's first experience in the cave was a painful realization of how far he had strayed. It was a time of reassessment. After acknowledging that he had enemies he could not defeat, circumstances that he could not fix, and an emptiness he could not fill, this was his prayer in Psalm 57:

> Please, God, show me mercy!
> Open your grace-fountain for me,
> for you are my soul's true shelter.
> I will hide beneath the shadow of your embrace,
> under the wings of your cherubim,
> until this terrible trouble is past.
> I will cry out to you, the God of the highest
> heaven,
> the mighty God, who performs all these won-
> ders for me.
> From heaven he will send a father's help to
> save me.
> He will trample down those who trample me.
> He will always show me love
> by his gracious and constant care.
> I am surrounded by these fierce and brutal men.
> They are like lions, just wanting to tear me to
> shreds.
> Why must I continue to live among these seeth-
> ing terrorists,
> breathing out their angry threats and insults
> against me?

Lord God, be exalted as you soar throughout
the heavens.
May your shining glory be seen in the skies!
Let it be seen high above over all the earth!
For they have set a trap for me.
Frantic fear has me overwhelmed.
But look! The very trap they set for me
has sprung shut upon themselves instead of me!
My heart, O God, is quiet and confident.
Now I can sing with passion your wonderful
praises!
Awake, O my soul, with the music of his splen-
dor-song!
Arise, my soul, and sing his praises!
My worship will awaken the dawn,
greeting the daybreak with my songs of praise!
Wherever I go I will thank you, my God.
Among all the nations they will hear my praise
songs to you.
Your love is so extravagant it reaches to the
heavens.
Your faithfulness so astonishing it stretches to
the sky!
Lord God, be exalted as you soar throughout
the heavens.
May your shining glory be shown in the skies!
Let it be seen high above all the earth! (TPT)

In Matthew 8, there is a great discourse between Jesus
and a Roman Centurion. The Centurion asked Jesus to
come and heal his sick son. His personal observation of Jesus had convinced him that He was so powerful He could

simply speak a command and his son would be healed. The authority to do such an amazing exploit was based upon his own personal years of training. True authority is the result of your own submission to authority.

The Centurion had quickly observed that Jesus was not operating rogue. Clearly, He was obedient to a higher authority. The Centurion's observation was revealed with this statement: "For I myself am a man under authority, with soldiers under me. I tell this one, 'Go,' and he goes; and that one, 'Come,' and he comes. I say to my servant, 'Do this,' and he does it" (Matt. 8:8-9 NIV).

This man had first-hand, experiential knowledge of the power and authority granted to those who have submitted to authority. His keen observation was that Jesus' total submission to a power much greater than Himself would surely result in possessing the power and authority to "say the word" and heal his son.

The point is this: if you want to have authority and influence in your world, you must be submitted to authority from another world.

Many men go through life as "rogue agents." No one can tell them what to do, and they will answer to no one. They have zero accountability or respect for any kind of authority. Then they become frustrated when family, friends, and everyone in their world fail to respect their masculinity. But if you're not submitting to God's authority, don't expect others to respond to you correctly.

In the beginning, God placed the man He had created in the Garden of Eden alone, all by himself. Adam was given dominion over everything God had created. We don't know the exact length of time before God brought

Eve to him, but we know it was a significant space of time—and that it was intentional.

Some people think that one day God suddenly realized that it was a mistake for Adam to be on earth by himself. But that's clearly not the way it happened. First of all, everything God does is perfect and complete—and intentional.

May I submit a different thought for you to consider? After God had created everything in the garden, He created Adam and gave him a special assignment. While alone with all of the other creatures, Adam was to have dominion over every living thing. And, of course, there were daily meetings when God would come into the garden and have conversations with Adam.

We don't know how long this lasted, but the reason seems clear enough. Before man could be trusted with a wife and a family, God first had to establish a precedent. If a man cannot effectively walk with his God, he is incapable of successfully leading a family. A mighty man has to establish and maintain a relationship with God before he can accomplish anything else.

I think this concept is as true today as it has ever been. Only when a man finds completeness in his Maker does he have the ability to knock it out of the park as a husband, father, and leader in his world.

A real man stands tallest when he's on his knees in prayer.

Real completeness can only be achieved by mastering your relationship with God. That does not mean it will be flawless with no need for improvement. It simply means that He has become first in your life! He is the one you worship; He's the strength you depend upon and the first One you go to for help. He's not just part of your life—He is the *center* of your life. When you're complete in Him, this is how it will affect you:

- A mature and consistent faith
- Unshakable and centered confidence
- Properly arranged priorities
- A healthy self-image
- Uncommon clarity of purpose
- Mastery of your emotions
- Maturity in your thought processes
- Control over all of your fleshly appetites
- Strong and healthy relationships in your life

This is an incredible list of characteristics and temperaments, but each can be an automatic byproduct of a life that has been fully surrendered to God. Putting Him first in everything means just that: in *everything*! He must come first; when He's in that "first" position, a redemptive quality rests upon everything else. Your time, your money, your health, your relationships, your mind, the overall rhythm of life—everything begins to work better!

Putting God first indiscriminately and without reservation is the highest possible priority for the complete man. Abiding by this law creates a perpetual effect that continues through the entire circle of a man's life.

David had to return to his first dependence upon God as a shepherd boy: those songs he composed of worship and praise; that supernatural strength that enveloped him when he defeated the lion and the bear; that powerful anointing that surged through his spirit when he shouted to the giant Goliath, "You come against me with sword and spear and javelin, but I come to you in the name of the LORD Almighty, the God of the armies of Israel" (1 Sam. 17:45 NIV).

It was time to return to the One who had called him out of obscurity, anointed him, favored him, and blessed him —the God who had somehow slipped beneath first place. As David approached that cave, what an awakening he felt in his soul. He immediately knew that if God wasn't first, he was finished!

Small-Group Discussion Points

- *Start assessing your priorities.* In which area has God slipped in your list of priorities? For many men, self-awareness has become a lost virtue. If you can't accurately "red-dot" where you are, you can't even begin to select the path you should follow. Evaluate where you are spending most of your time and money.
- *Make some new commitments to your faith community.* You can't declare that God is first then neglect the things He cares about most. A sure sign that God is first in your life is when the things that matter most to Him matter most to you. Attending church every Sunday should be a "non-negotiable."
- *Start practicing generosity toward God with your finances.* Where you spend money is where you're directing your heart. If you're unable

to honor God with your money, you may have backed yourself into a corner by over-spending. This could be a great opportunity to discover why it happened. How did a boat become more important than honoring God? Which investments have pulled you away from being consistently faithful to God?

5

Father Fractures

It's no coincidence that after returning to God, the first thing David planned was a reunion with his family (1 Sam. 22:1). The embarrassment and rejection of his father and the conflict with his brothers had to be resolved.

Consider this: after making God first in their lives, the first issue the cave dwellers addressed was fatherhood. Whether their father had been absent, disconnected, disengaged, abusive, or indifferent, the fractures were still there.

This will be the longest chapter of this book since it is, without question, a core issue with every man. The problem of fatherlessness in our culture has been rampant for at least three decades. That means that most of us were produced by a father who had also grown up without a father. It's time to bring generations of perpetual dysfunction to an end.

Just about every negative thing in your life—your weaknesses, your internal/emotional conflicts, your insecurities, wanderings, identity struggles, personality flaws, etc.—are the result of what we call a "father fracture." In other words, almost all negative behavior, instability, and emotional immaturity are the result of father issues in the earliest stages of our lives. The phrase "father fracture" is not originally mine. Many experts who have written about these issues have used this phrase. Since I cannot pinpoint the person who coined it first, we'll just agree that it's an adequate phrase that has often been used to describe a very unfortunate reality. These fathers who have been absent (or at least disconnected and disengaged) did not realize the impact of their absence.

Most would agree that God's perfect plan is for every child to grow up with the guidance, love, wisdom, and godly example of a good father and mother who will prepare him or her to successfully navigate their way through the entirety of life. While the entire focus of this book is upon the father, that does not mean that the mother's role is any less significant.

In fact, I should pause here long enough to congratulate the mothers and the women in our lives that did NOT abandon us. The need to write a book like this, which is specifically to and about men, does not dismiss the role of the women in our lives. To the contrary, I thank God for the women who have done a stellar job in carrying such a tremendous load by themselves. Confronting the epidemic of fatherlessness in this world does not diminish the value and role of women and mothers. There are equally significant (or perhaps worse) developmental challenges in the lives of those who grow up motherless and those who grow up fatherless. The plain hard truth is simply, by and large, women have not disappeared like so many men have. It is far less likely that a mother would perpetrate neglect or abandonment concerning a child than a man. It does happen, but not nearly as often as with men. Perhaps it has something to do with the nature of nurturing.

But I turn my attention back to the subject at hand. I have my personal assignment: to teach and facilitate men coming to Jesus and repairing the father fractures.

During the span of every man's life, and at every stage of his development, there are reasonable expectations for what he should experience, develop, and achieve. This is true throughout our lives, but most critically during the very first years.

Here are some of the expectations and factors that have been pre-wired into our subconscious:

- The need for affirmation of our identity
- The need to be believed in
- The need to be loved
- How to embrace our uniqueness
- How to love and treat women in all contexts (sisters, mothers, wives, aunts, etc.)
- How to handle adversity and conflict
- The premise of our worldview
- The assurance that we're valued and approved

This list could go on and on, and there is another list that must be addressed by the mother, but these are the most basic and critical factors in the context of a boy and his father. In simple and innocent ways, these needs are met in a healthy relationship between a father and his son. And for reasons known only to God, it seems that is the only way they can be met—by a father who is present, interactive, and engaged.

The father provides the gendering while the mother provides the nurturing. Men determine the sex of a baby based on whether their sperm is carrying an X or Y chromosome. An X chromosome combines with the mother's X chromosome to make a baby girl (XX), and a Y chromosome will combine with the mother's X chromosome to make a boy (XY). That continues throughout life; the mother provides the nurturing, and the father provides the gendering. Gendering simply means that the man holds a lot of power to affirm his sons and daughters to be the young men and women that God created them to be.

In a culture where the overwhelming majority of males are growing up without the presence of their father, this has become a problem of epic proportions. Even in homes where the father was present, many still missed the element of being engaged and interactive. This reality has lasted so long that the idea of fatherhood for most men was inadvertently taught to them by a father who had himself been raised fatherless. That makes three generations of men who have endured this reality.

I realize that we all live in a fallen world with a certain amount of adversity to deal with, but for those of us who grew up with a "Dad issue," the problem is much bigger and more complex than the norm—and much more difficult to overcome.

First, I want to talk about fathers who are engaged, attentive, and interactive with their sons, fathers who understand the necessity of their role in their son's young life. I think we'd agree that while fathers are needed throughout our lives, they are most needed during our earliest stages of development.

When Jesus was baptized, as He came up out of the water, the voice of His Father resounded from heaven: "This is my beloved Son, in whom I am well pleased" (Matt. 3:17 KJV). That was the Father's way of affirming His Son.

Ironically, Jesus was immediately driven into the wilderness by the Spirit to be tempted by the devil. "If You are the Son of God ..." was the preface of the three worst temptations the devil could throw at Him. It's no coincidence that just hours before Jesus' wilderness experience, the Father felt it was necessary to once again affirm Jesus' identity. If Jesus, the Son of God, needed this affirmation, I'm sure it must be important for every one of us.

There are a number of meaningful analyses of the masculine stages of development from birth to the golden years. While the descriptions vary, they all seem to agree that there are some very distinct stages, each with its own rite of passage to the next.

In his book, *Wild at Heart*, John Eldridge identifies six stages: Boyhood, Cowboy, Warrior, Lover, King, and Sage. In Robert Hicks' book, *The Masculine Journey*, he mentions six stages, as well. Similarly, in Gordon Dalbey's brilliant book, Healing the Masculine Soul, he also defines six stages, but with different names. We can all agree that the masculine soul develops in stages, each with its own experience and objective. We should all have certain experiences, discoveries, and affirmations that will prepare us for the next level of growth.

Each stage builds on the assumption that every need was successfully addressed in the previous stage. If we miss an affirmation or experience, there's a flawed basis upon which to build the next stage. Such flaws rarely adjust themselves or become whole or complete over a period of time. Each of them can breed a much worse and more complex deficiency.

Unfortunately, in my personal experience and in the hundreds of men I have mentored or counseled, these flaws and deficiencies can be permanent. Somehow, they are buried just beneath the surface of our life, always ready to sabotage our future. Still worse, they are usually repeated in our sons.

At some point, we must grow tired of arriving at a new stage, door, or opportunity feeling unequipped to maximize the new chapter we are about to begin. An older man may find ways to compensate or work around his deficiencies in a later stage, but that is seldom true for younger men.

The dilemma is that a young boy innocently troops through childhood, completely unaware of what he should be taught by his father and, therefore, unaware of what he's missing—that is until he's a grown man trying to figure out why he's the way he is. This is precisely why most men advance much faster in age than they do in maturity. Culture can attempt to redefine normal as much as it wants, but it will never change the essential needs our Creator has wired into us as young men.

Briefly, let's look at the absolute essentials a young boy needs from his father. While it would seem that the "boyhood" stage is relatively carefree and filled with discovery, adventure, games, and fun, there are still some intangibles that cannot be ignored. Between the ages (the range is still up for debate) of learning to walk and the awkward preteen years, these are some indelible impressions in a young man that will likely never change or be removed:

- The premise of his worldview
- The affirmation of his identity
- His perspective on the innocence of life
- His assurance of being loved
- How women are to be treated
- How it feels to be believed in
- And a host of other affirmations

The deficiencies that we call "wounds" or "fractures" are almost impossible to overcome due to two primary facts: we will never again be as impressionable or innocent as we were as a child. And after we have been beaten up by life, we become more cynical about those fundamental truths. But there's still hope!

It is important to remember that God is unlike anyone you have ever known. He is a perfect Father. Psalm 68:5 (KJV) says, "A father of the fatherless, and a judge of the widows, is God in his holy habitation."

Think about that for a moment. Only God, who is not limited by time or space, can take us back to those moments when we were so deeply affected by fatherlessness and make all those wrongs right. He has promised to take up the slack and heal our father fractures. Whatever your father should have done or said to you but did not, God can offer—and will. The affirmations you should have received but did not, God can and will provide—right now!

I must pause here to warn against the notion that in this world, there could be a perfect father. There is not. It certainly is not wise to hold our fathers to some unrealistic standard or expectation. If all of humanity had begun with your father, then perhaps you could hold him totally responsible. But it did not. Your father followed the script that had been handed to him by his father, that had been handed to him by his father, and so on. Of course, many of our situations are more severe than others. But this principle is not confined to guys who are messed up because of their dysfunctional dads. Even if you had a stellar father, you could still have "father fractures" simply because the best fathers among us are still flawed and imperfect.

Our earthly fathers are but a glimpse into true fatherhood. Therefore, incompleteness as a father doesn't merit shame or condemnation. Our fathers are given to us to provoke/instigate an appetite for our heavenly Father.

Neither would I suggest that a negative father situation was intentional. Under the best of circumstances, we can get it wrong as fathers. We have done the best we knew to do and tried to teach our sons how to be men by pointing them to our perfect Heavenly Father. But we must realize that there's no such thing as a dad who aced it. God promised to be a Father to the fatherless, knowing full well that every man growing up in this fallen world would have some degree of dysfunction. Because of man's fallen state, *no* father does the perfect thing all the time.

Going back to those men who are really struggling, let's not forget that we live in a very broken world. One that has all but completely turned its back on God's principles. This abandonment of Divine law has resulted in so many conditions that are conducive to father dysfunction. Pre-marital births, incarcerations, and outright abandonment are just a few of the factors that contribute to the epidemic of father-lessness. Additionally, fathers are often involuntarily relegated by family courts to the role of an "accessory parent" rather than an active caregiver. Mutual parental discord can also put kids on the table as "bargaining chips" or tools of vengeance.

Whether our problem is the result of intentional abandonment, outright rejection, absence, abuse, disengagement, or simply a shortcoming by a well-meaning dad, men must deal with these issues that stem from a flawed dad relationship.

The experts in the behavioral science community have correlated many social dynamics with fatherlessness. Here are a few of them:

- *Emotionally unresponsive*: If deprived of strong masculine energy in your childhood, you could have adopted the pseudo-idea of masculinity from pop culture or sports/entertainment figures as the pattern for emotional connection. When an emotionally charged situation occurs, it's difficult for the father-fractured man to deal with it. He is more likely to think, "I don't need this right now. I will deal with this stuff later."
- *Four times more likely to wrestle with poverty.* While this may seem a bit mysterious, statistics affirm that poverty is inexplicably linked to fatherlessness. A home with an absentee father quickly reveals how the family's priorities have been misplaced.

- *Transfers blame to others instead of taking ownership of the problem.* Someone's coping mechanism is very flawed if they blame someone else for their own emotional conflict. When a man does not feel equipped or capable of taking responsibility, he is quick to lash out at others. Suddenly, he has become the victim, and everyone else is the problem.
- *Becomes extremely angry about minuscule events and is likely to blame others for their inappropriate display of anger.* "She made me angry." "They drove me to it." "Look what they made me do." These are the kinds of statements a father-fractured man will lean toward.
- *In a "relationship" with a spouse, but with several other "options" on the side.* Similar to the tendency of hoarding after the scarcity of the Great Depression, fractured men are afraid to invest 100% of themselves for fear they could lose everything at any minute. After watching good people leave at the worst possible time, their safest bet is to loosely entertain "options."
- *Does not know how to be intimate and close unless it involves sex.* If a man does not know how to have an honorable and respectful interaction with a woman, he only knows how to resort to "base instincts."
- *Self-esteem issues: always feels driven to "prove" himself.* If not approved or appreciated by others, he will quickly become angry.

- *Constant need for being accepted and approved.* The fractured man's craving for attention often results in risky behavior or criminal conduct. He finds it hard to distinguish between healthy attention and becoming a spectacle.
- *Difficulty in bonding, even with his own children.* After growing up without much significant bonding, he does not know where to begin. He often just crosses his fingers and hopes his family will turn out well.
- *More likely to experience depression and anxiety from a lack of coping skills and examples of healthy conflict resolution.*

The comparisons are almost endless. Juvenile, delinquent, self-sabotaging behaviors will raise their ugly heads over and over again at the worst possible times. It's enough to make a man feel as though life is nothing more than a circular journey through one "almost" after another! *I almost had it; I was almost wealthy; I almost had a great marriage; I got really close to happiness,* and so on. To most guys, it feels like the normal circle of life is unchangeable. So, just do the best you can and get whatever you can. But that is so wrong! God has so much more for you in the cave—you have to get there!

How to Fix the Father Fracture

What does it all mean? Does your father need a reset? Should he apologize? Do you need to "fix" him and hold him accountable for his mistakes? I would say "no" to all of these.

What we need most is to throw ourselves at the feet of Jesus and allow our perfect Heavenly Father to heal whatever is broken.

Undoubtedly, God knew David needed to resolve some things before he could emerge from the cave and begin to rule. There were many fatherless characteristics in his life, so let's take a closer look at the relationship between David and his father.

- In Psalm 51:5 (KJV), David said: "Behold I was shapen in iniquity; and in sin did my mother conceive me." While this doctrine is not a settled fact, it's certainly worth considering when you observe David's behavior as a grown man. There has always been a mystery about the identity of his mother. Her name is never mentioned.
- When Samuel asked Jesse to call all of his sons together, they were all called but one— David. The prophet had to press Jesse to bring his other son or to even admit that one more was in the pasture.
- Is it possible that David was the fruit of a mistake made by Jesse? Was David's presence a reminder of his father's transgression? Many Jewish scholars believe that David was the product of an inappropriate sexual relationship between Jesse and David's mother.
- Why, on this incredibly rare and special occasion when the prophet of the land comes to your home, would you fail to bring one son to this event?

- Many Jewish Rabbis believe this is the reason David was constantly rejected by his father and relegated to one of the lowest tasks in the family. Much of the time, he was banished to the pasture.
- His brothers also resented him and did not welcome his presence.
- King Saul, who became a father figure to David and eventually his father-in-law, turned on him and even tried to kill him multiple times.

Those are some pretty heavy father issues. Perhaps they are contributing factors to the fact that throughout David's psalms and prayers, he was incessantly concerned that God would leave or forsake him. The references are too numerous to mention, but read through the Psalms sometime with this thought in mind. David constantly made comments such as:

- Please don't hide your face from me.
- Cast me not away.
- Don't leave me alone.
- Please don't forsake me.
- Don't hide yourself from me.

The references are constant. Is it possible that David's "I've got this" attitude stemmed from the fact that he was trying to feel his way through an anointing that his father Jesse had never known? Is it possible that David's alarming experiences with his new mentor, King Saul, produced so much more rejection and abandonment that he began to transfer his fears to God?

Why was David so often worried that God might leave or forsake him? Could it have come from the flawed father model during all his childhood years? I can totally relate, and perhaps you can, as well.

This is the most damaging and lasting consequence of fatherlessness—transferred hostility and suspicion. We men tend to see God through the lens of our own experiences with our earthly fathers. Whatever impressions we have of earthly fatherhood, those perceptions become our attitude toward our heavenly Father. Our fear of divine abandonment comes from our personal experiences, not to mention the depth of our ability to trust and depend on God.

Many of our fathers overreacted to our mistakes from a lack of resolving their own conflicts. Perhaps the gift you possess was so foreign to your father he did not know how to instruct or guide you. Maybe he was repeating the patterns he had observed in his childhood. Whatever the case, you will have to encounter God for yourself to understand that our perfect Heavenly Father will never leave nor forsake you but will be with you to the very end.

Psalms 68:5 (KJV): "A father to the fatherless...is God in his holy habitation." Getting correctly aligned with your heavenly Father will produce a father consciousness that will manifest through you to your future generations.

The prophet Elijah asked his successor one day what he wanted most. For years Elisha had followed Elijah around and treated him like a father figure. Elijah the mentor, training and raising up the mentee. Elisha answered, "Let me inherit a double portion of your spirit" (2 Kings 2:9 NIV). The father/prophet said, "If you see me when I am taken from you, it will be yours" (2 Kings 2:10 KJV). Just imagine how closely Elisha must have followed Elijah. There won't be any warning or advance notice. I'm sure Elisha never let Elijah out of his sight. Imagine how attentive Elisha was to observe the life and movement of his mentor.

I think it's quite possible that Elijah was purposely emphasizing not so much the moment of his departure but rather the necessary closeness of their relationship leading up to it.

When Elijah was taken up into heaven in a fiery chariot by a whirlwind, the mantle he had worn throughout his life floated down to his successor Elisha. As soon as Elisha touched it, he proclaimed, "My father! My father!" (2 Kings 2:12 NIV). That mantle represented a double portion of the very anointing and power Elisha had asked for. There's something about an encounter with Father God that raises the awareness of true fatherhood in a man. An exponential increase of power occurs when you get aligned with the heart and character of your heavenly Father. It is further understood that the revelation of the benefits of our heavenly Father can be shown to us through an earthly father. Such was the case with Elisha. Elijah had shown him the value of fatherhood, and when he realized the extent of the double portion he had received, he exclaimed, "My father! My father!" (2 Kings 2:12 NIV). Twice.

Skipping forward, David seemed to know that these dangerous circumstances must end, or it would be the end of him. Realizing the magnitude of trouble and danger for his family, the first thing he did was secure a safe place for his mother and father. What an example of "honoring thy father and thy mother, that it may go well with you and your days may be long on the earth" (Exod. 20:12 KJV).

The next thing he did was bring his brothers into the cave with him. The brothers who had publicly resented and belittled him, expressed cruel jealousy, and were a big part of David's childhood rejection issues? Yes, those brothers. They needed a cave, too. He probably suspected they had their own issues to overcome, and there was no better place than the cave of Adullam.

If you're relating to the reality of a father fracture, let me end this chapter with these simple instructions.

Small-Group Discussion Points

- *Forgive your father.* That does not mean you have to "feel" it. Forgiveness is objective rather than emotional. It will also help you separate your personal pain from his mistreatment and release it. In time, you'll learn to effectively feel it, but not right now. If you wait to "feel" forgiveness, you'll never extend it. Justified or not, your father had his own reasons for his actions, or perhaps his own private demons to deal with. Most likely, it's all unknown to you, just as it may have even been unknown to him. This is what Jesus said: "Father, forgive them; for they know not what they do" (Luke 23:34 KJV). When you forgive, you must surrender your personal demand for justice to a God who knows how to deal with it. Let people off your hook and onto God's hook so you can be free.

- *Pray for your father.* If he's still living and it's possible, the most powerful and liberating way is to pray for him in person. If that's not possible, pray anyway. Ask God to let you see your father through His eyes of mercy and compassion. Gordon Dalbey says, "A little boy cries FROM his father's wounds, but a healed man cries FOR his father's wounds." Even if he has passed from this life, seeing him in a different way will affect your conversations about him. It will also build your character as a man.
- *Honor your father.* To honor him does not condone his actions or the way he treated you. It merely taps into and releases your own God-given ability to do good when it's neither merited nor deserved. This is God's way. In fact, it's what He did for you. Honor your father by changing the way you refer to him and remembering what he has done for you.
- *Thank God for your mentors.* My father loved this old saying and used it often: "If you ever see a turtle sitting on top of a pole, you can safely assume someone put it there." A turtle can't climb a pole by itself. If you're going to be free and healed, you will need mentors to help you get there. Search for mentors who can present new models of fatherhood. Since there are seven different dimensions of life, no father can be perfect or all-encompassing. That's why you need more than one earthly example of fatherhood. You need a mentor

for business and money, for family and inter-
personal relationships, for intellect and emotions, health and fitness, and other protocols
of masculinity.

- *Commit your masculinity to God.* In Psalm 31:5
  (NIV), David said, "Into your hands I commit my spirit." Most people think of that
  statement as Jesus' last words on the cross
  when He said, "Father, into Your hands I
  commit my spirit" (Luke 23:46 NIV). But
  Jewish scholars refer to this as a staple prayer
  of young Jewish boys. Every night before
  bed, this is the prayer they speak to God. It
  means: "Heavenly Father, I commit the wellbeing of my fragile spirit to You. If there's
  any slack or deficiency, I trust that You will
  safeguard me and make up the difference."
  This is a great way to commit the fragility of
  our masculinity to our perfect Heavenly Father.

- *Continue developing new patterns.* Lasting
  change does not come quickly or easily.
  Along the way, you will have challenges and
  setbacks. Start paying attention to those reoc-
  curring behavior patterns that are self-de-
  structive and self-sabotaging. You may not
  be everything you want to be, but you're far
  from where you once were. Give yourself
  some grace and some time. It takes a while to
  develop and stick to this new narrative of
  life. As my father used to say, "Long-term

obedience in the same direction will always get you a payday."

6

Give Up and Get Up!

If you're like the overwhelming majority of men in our world, you have plenty of disappointments and deficiencies in your father/son relationship. But it's important to remember that our fathers were also flawed and imperfect. Most of them were living according to the script that had been handed to them.

If you want to make great strides in your quest to become a mighty and complete man, you have to let everyone who came before you off the hook. If you're expecting grace to set you free and propel you forward, you'll have to extend that same grace to others. You cannot be the great executor of justice for everyone else. You're not responsible for seeing that everyone 'pays' or gets what's coming to them. It's up to you to move onward and upward. And the absolute requirement is for you to "give up!"

As they say, you can't just quit or roll over and play dead. But you must give up the desire to punish and correct everyone else's wrongs. Give it up—and let God do whatever is needed.

If you want to get up and move up, you will have to give up.

Those in your past may have done you wrong. The ones who were shooting at you and trying to pull you down may be the very ones who should have been cheering you on. Perhaps those who hurt you should have been helping you.

Many of us have had our share of terrible disappointments. All of us men have had people turn their backs on us at the worst possible times. We've been betrayed by people who were very close to us. But holding on to any of that does not help. Every man must reach the point where his only concern is this: *"What do I have to do to get free, get healed, and get on top where I belong?"*

Let's look again at the transformation timeline while David was in Adullam's cave. Scripture tells us that his purpose for going to the cave was to hide from his enemies. Absolutely as low as he could go, his first prayers in the cave were repentance and crying out to God for salvation. Both prayers are recorded in Psalm 57 and Psalm 142.

When his family heard about David, they joined him. But how did they know where he was hiding? Is it possible that he told them? During his time of repentance and transformation, he must have recognized the importance of gathering his family around him. You mean those jealous brothers who had rejected him and the father who was too embarrassed and ashamed to even call David his son? Yes, that family!

But this was not the time for revenge. No one had to pay or offer groveling apologies. It was simply time to give up so he could heal up and get up! This is why David could be trusted to lead this group of 400 transformed men.

Let the world off the hook. Since you're not the
great equalizer, you can't settle all the scores.
Don't allow the pain of your past to drive you.
The purpose of God is your fuel.

I can assure you that David did not allow their excuses and blame game to last very long in the cave. At some point, their focus had to turn to their mission and the changes that would qualify these men for it. The words of Lao Tzu are again appropriate: *"He who conquers others is strong; He who conquers himself is mighty."*

Only those who will risk going too far can
possibly find out how far one can go.
—T. S. Eliot

It was time to face the reality of the moment. Outside the cave, there was a substantial number of enemies who meant them great harm. Since the men were still ill-equipped and had nothing to go back to, leaving the cave would be devastating. Before they could face whatever was outside the cave, they had to conquer themselves. All their excuses were empty and meaningless.

It is better to offer no excuse than a bad one.
—George Washington

The best place to begin was self-mastery. I can almost hear David, their experienced leader, standing to say:

"Gentlemen, repeat this after me—and then repeat it often, every day:

- I'm a grown man.
- My own decisions/reactions are the reason I'm here.
- I have no excuses to offer.
- My friends are not listening, and my enemies don't care.
- It's not my fault, but I am still responsible.
- Nobody else is going to come to my rescue.
- Enough is enough.
- Today, I'm taking back my future.
- I am good enough to change.
- I have the power to change.
- My family deserves a better me.
- I'm no longer going to be driven by my pain.
- Purpose is my new compass.
- God is not against me.
- God is for me.
- I was born for this time and this purpose.
- Since God is for me, no one can stop me but me."

And he may have gone on and on, reinforcing the fact that these grown men must move beyond being broke, stressed out, and unhappy. It was time to give up their past hurts and injustices. All their excuses, ideals, and thought processes would have to change. The bad patterns that had led them there must be replaced. This *must* happen for them to leave the cave as "the Mighty."

More injustices would come later. They would still have to endure rejection and betrayal. Not everyone would cheer them on. Life has a way of throwing disappointments in our path, along with a defeat or two. But after the cave, it would be different. They were healed and connected to their purpose. Their posture and perspectives were different because they had persevered. They had worked harder on mastering themselves than ever before. Enduring a painful and grueling experience had totally transformed them. Hiding in a cave had become a metamorphosis experience. This is how they had become *the Mighty*.

I have missed more than 9,000 shots in my career. I have lost almost 300 games. I have been trusted to take the winning game 26 times—and missed! I have failed over and over and over in my life. And that is why I succeed.
—Michael Jordan

Small-Group Discussion Points

- *Make the necessary phone calls or visits to the people who have been the source of much pain in your life.* But don't be harsh, judgmental, or corrective. That's not the way of the cave. Instead, just let them off the hook.
- *Give the need for justice, retribution, and vengeance to God.* He's the only one who is qualified to handle it.

- *In your daily devotion, mention the fact that you are releasing everyone and everything you've been holding onto.* Ask God to heal your emotions. Believe that eventually, the internal hurt will be replaced by an unstoppable resolve to keep moving upward.
- Multiple times a day, declare that you are "giving up so you can get healed up and can get up."

7

Imago Dei / Ikonea Theos

At some point in this transformation experience, you must begin to understand your "God-likeness." Genesis 1:27 (KJV) says, "So God created man in His own image, in the image of God created he him." These two terms merit a closer look.

- *Image of God:* "*Imago dei*" refers to the similarity of our ability, creativity, knowledge, and reason to His. Man was created with God-like abilities in our posture and our ability to reign with Him.
- *Likeness of God:* "*Ikonea theos*" refers to His nature, character, authority, and presence.

Adam was created with both the image and likeness of God. When he disobeyed and was cast out of the Garden, he did not lose the image of God. Instead, he forfeited the "likeness" of God.

Spoiler alert: the great news is that Jesus came to restore all that Adam had lost. When we conform to Christ's example, the likeness of God is restored.

A man is morally lazy until something captures his heart.

Discovering your purpose begins with the realization that you were created in God's image. That means something. In fact, it means everything! The simple explanation is that man was created to resemble God (not to be a god) and to possess God-like qualities and abilities. This sets us apart from the rest of creation and equips us to responsibly rule over all the earth.

From the beginning, this God-like stewardship of creation was wired into man. No other created thing can boast of such a quality. Once you realize that the same God who created you in His image and likeness had a specific reason for doing so, you're well on your way to discovering your purpose.

First, you must acknowledge that you're not here to just bounce from one idea, project, or passion to another or to find your own way. Our lives were meant to be in perfect alignment with a definitive purpose and master plan for the entirety of life. This issue is so critical that it should be at the top of your quest for knowledge. The secret to discovering your purpose is to realize that it's not rooted in personal achievement but a spiritual inheritance. This is whom God created you to be in the beginning.

To be created in God's image refers to each person's posture and ability. He has positioned and equipped us with all the necessary components to fulfill the plan He designed for us. But is it enough to merely believe in *imago dei*? Isn't it enough to be equipped with God-like qualities and abilities so we can fulfill our dominion? Maybe that's what David was thinking. Wouldn't supernaturally killing lions, bears, and giants confirm your God-like ability to exercise dominion? Somewhere along the way, he must have realized that supernatural skill, ability, and power would cause him trouble if he never experienced a restoration of God's likeness or *ikonea theos*. He was still missing that sameness of heart and character with the One who had given him those marvelous abilities.

Notice what David wrote in Psalm 17:15 (NKJV): "As for me, I will see Your face in righteousness; I shall be satisfied when I awake in Your likeness."

Perhaps he finally became aware that focusing on power, authority, and outright supernatural ability had been at the expense of his intimate relationship with God as a boy. Something had changed — and it needed to change again!

The challenge for many men is that they may have the power, ability, and gifting to rise to the top, but if they don't have "likeness," they will lack the ability to sustain it. Your gifting and charisma cannot outgrow your likeness to God.

Your gifting is closely connected to the *imago dei*, but there is more. A man's clarity of purpose must stem from an intimate relationship with God. From the beginning, God's plan was to form such an inseparable partnership with man that His divine attributes would become our human virtues. When His glorious image and power are reflected through us, we are fulfilling His design for us.

The internal longing in every man is to know precisely why he is here and what he should be accomplishing. The answer to this question is crucial to transformation. Job 36:5 (NIV) says, "God is mighty, but despises no one; he is mighty, and firm in his purpose." Therefore, my brother, you should do the same: *become firm in your purpose!*

In his initial state of innocence, man resembled God morally (in his thoughts), socially (we were made for fellowship), and spiritually. Part of that reality was man's freedom to make choices.

Although Adam, the first man, and his wife, Eve, were created with innocence, they chose to rebel against their Creator. The result was not a loss of *imago dei*—it was their "God-likeness" or "same-ness" that was damaged and marred.

The good news is that when a man looks to Jesus Christ as his perfect example, his original God-likeness begins to be reinstated. Once again, he returns to that righteous and holy image of God.

The Son is the image of the invisible God, the firstborn over all creation. (Col. 1:15 NIV)

In the above verse, image means likeness or sameness. Simply stated, if every aspect of your life is modeled after Jesus, you are conforming to that original *ikonea theos*. Since you were born in the image of God, you're already pre-wired for dominion. But like David, your pride, ego, and stubbornness can keep you from operating in purpose.

Without that "likeness," a man will bounce around, doing any and everything he thinks he has the ability to do. And for the most part, he's right. The more gifted and talented you are, the greater the temptation. There may be many things you are able to do in your lifetime, but there is only *one* thing you were specifically created to do. Finding that *one* thing will produce an unprecedented measure of fulfillment and success in your life. That kind of clarity comes from a closeness with God. To know exactly what you're supposed to do with all of your amazing abilities, you must draw near to the heart of God.

Losing your "sameness" or "likeness" to God is like the parable of the lost lamb. That one lamb kept straying away from the flock, refusing to conform to what was best for it. Or perhaps it was just too adventurous for its own good. Luke 15:4-6 tells us that God is like that good shepherd.

> What man of you, having a hundred sheep, if he loses one of them, does not leave the ninety-nine in the wilderness, and go after the one which is lost until he finds it? And when he has found *it*, he lays *it* on his shoulders, rejoicing. And when he comes home, he calls together *his* friends and neighbors, saying to them, 'Rejoice with me, for I have found my sheep which was lost!'

When a good shepherd finds the sheep that has strayed, he places it upon his shoulders, close to his heart and close enough for the sheep to become more familiar with his voice. A sheep that recognizes the heart and voice of its shepherd will not stray.

So it is with men. We must become familiar with the heart of our heavenly Father and learn to recognize and, above all, *trust* His voice. That kind of closeness will give you an uncommon clarity of purpose.

Consideration and discontinuation of certain activities, associations, and pursuits may be in order for you. But when you're doing what you were created to do with the power and ability you were created to possess, you'll become unstoppable.

That's what these guys learned in the cave. Broken, distressed, and defeated guys became the mighty! Undoubtedly, the atmosphere in the cave was more than simply hanging out with other guys under a blanket of secrecy. They had learned to dwell in a secret place with God and experience a restoration of *ikonea theos*. Out of that closeness with God came clarity concerning their purpose: fight for your family and your land!

Small-Group Discussion Points

- *Repentance should always be included in your daily devotion.* Tell God you're sorry for thinking your gifts and abilities are more important than your character.
- *Declare that you were made in the image of God.* It's not a matter of pitting image and likeness against each other, nor is it an either/or scenario. To be one of the mighty, both are absolutely necessary.
- *Thank God every day that Jesus made it possible for you to be restored to His likeness.* Ask for His help to know Him better, to know His heart, and to recognize His voice. Spend time in the secret place every day, drawing closer to the Father.
- *Put Jesus first. Read about Him and consider His ways.* Ask yourself how He would handle a particular challenge or situation in your life.

- *Continue leaning in toward God during those intimate times of prayer and worship.* You are never closer to being like Him than when you are in His presence, worshiping and meditating upon Him.
- *Make Christ's character and nature a higher priority than the gifts and abilities He has given you.* Your gifts are not going anywhere, nor will they diminish. As you conform to the image of Jesus, your gifts will only increase.

8

Tend to Your Garden

A good rule of thumb for discovering your purpose is to have total clarity concerning the ultimate outcome of your life and your next step. Nothing in between is critical, so don't sweat it.

Now, let's break this down a bit. Genesis 1 gives us a broad overview of why man was created: to have dominion over all the earth and every created thing upon it.

Chapter 2 breaks it into even smaller, bite-sized pieces. After God had created the heavens and the earth, He created the Garden of Eden. This beautiful, pristine place did not resemble other parts of the undeveloped planet. This garden was a prototype for the rest of the earth. Then He created man and placed him in the middle of this garden.

> Now no shrub had yet appeared on the earth and no plant had yet sprung up, for the LORD God had not sent rain on the earth and there was no one to work the ground. (Gen. 2:5 NIV)

Adam, the first man, was given two primary responsibilities: The Garden of Eden and the rest of the world.

Garden (*gan*) means "an enclosed, protected, and sheltered place." Eden (*eden*) means "a place of delight, of pleasure, and of bliss."

Man was assigned to watch over this garden and keep it productive, beautiful, and healthy. Everything required for man's sustenance, fulfillment, and pleasure was found within the garden.

Then Adam was told to make the rest of the world look like Eden. Other parts of the world were to mirror man's success with Eden. This would naturally occur if he took his responsibilities seriously. Tend to this garden, protect it, and make it more fruitful.

Pretty simple, right? Rule over the whole earth, using Eden as a prototype. So how does a mighty man imitate this dominion or purpose?

Dominion and purpose must begin in the home. This is your Eden!

Your family and home are where every man's purpose begins. *First* and *foremost*, you are called to lead your queen and your family to follow after Jesus. To model what "Christ-followship" looks like, you must lovingly lead them to respond.

This will not be accomplished by some archaic, caveman attitude. To rule or exercise dominion is best understood in the concept of *headship*. Faith in Christ will restore the mighty man's God-like rule, taking him from an authoritative machismo rule over his wife and home to helping his wife and family follow God.

In Matthew 20:26 (NIV), Jesus compares the earthly concept of ruling with the kingdom concept. Worldly leaders rule by force, but Jesus warned, "Not so with you. Instead, whoever wants to become great among you must be your servant."

Headship is the man's specific and unique task of establishing order for all humanity. Once established and understood, it is exhibited first in the home, at church, and then in culture. It is amazing how clear things become and how almost effortless life is when man turns his heart toward his queen and his family.

We have been created by God for this purpose: to fight for the glory of God, for the soul of our queen, and for the development and protection of our tribe.

Dominion was given to mankind as a dual partnership between men and women, but the headship was given to the man. This was not intended to be subordination or subjugation. Neither does this distinction suggest inequality; headship simply means source or first. Adam was the first to be created from the dust, and then Eve was created from Adam.

God has not made or established covenant relationships directly with every individual on the earth; He has only done that with certain people. Then, in those covenants, He has made provision for inclusion for all humans. Others are included in these covenant relationships—either by God extending the covenant to them or linking them to that person He originally made a covenant with. Everyone who was linked to the covenant person received the same benefits and blessings of the covenant. This is the role of the head or the "mediator."

God made a covenant with Abraham. Then the inclusion factor was with Abraham's future generations, or his seed. Consequently, every Jewish person is included in the benefits of the covenant God made with Abraham.

God made a covenant with His son Jesus. The inclusion factor is at play with every human being that is "in Christ."

> For there is one mediator between God and mankind, the man Christ Jesus. (1 Tim. 2:5 NIV)

> For if, by the trespass of the one man, death reigned through that one man, how much more will those who receive God's abundant provision of grace and of the gift of righteousness reign in life through the one man, Jesus Christ! (Rom. 5:17 NIV)

Consider this: if God made a new covenant with His own Son, Jesus Christ, and Jesus is the mediator of that covenant, God's covenant is not with every single person on earth; it's with Jesus. Through Jesus, every blessing, advantage, favor, and covenant benefit has been extended to every human being. So, if we have surrendered our lives to Jesus, we are included in that covenant. That is the amazing power and absolute necessity of having a mediator!

In a similar sense, a man must not rule as a dictator over his wife and family. He is to walk in covenant with Jesus. By doing so as the head of his house, he will bring his entire family into the same blessing. As he models his submission to God to his family, he can lovingly lead them to respond in kind.

At first, it may seem that you're only the stopgap for everything that's negative, destructive, and hurtful coming against your family, always absorbing the stress and negativity aimed at your home. Instead, focus on the fact that you've been wonderfully assigned to be the entry point for everything that is good, righteous, favorable, virtuous, and blessed. Since you are the key to God's blessings and favor upon your family and home, your godly leadership is crucial.

The fruit of healthy headship is not fear or intimidation. Rather, headship has been entrusted to the man so that he can provide:

- A positive and Godly spiritual climate
- Clear spiritual direction
- A covering of protection
- The blessing of abundant provision

The favor and blessings of God upon your family are dependent upon your leadership as a man.

Headship strives for God's rule, while patriarchy strives for male rule. In His humanity, Jesus demonstrated the same leadership role that had been given to Adam. Jesus is the head of the mediator role and the king of a restored kingdom whose citizens willingly obey. Having all authority in heaven and earth, Jesus rules with authority, but not as a patriarchal ruler.

- John 5:19 (ESV): "So Jesus said to them, 'Truly, truly, I say to you, the Son can do nothing of his own accord, but only what he sees the Father doing. For whatever the Father does, that the Son does likewise.'"
- John 5:30 (ESV): "I can do nothing on my own. As I hear, I judge, and my judgment is just, because I seek not my own will but the will of him who sent me."
- John 6:38 (ESV): "For I have come down from heaven, not to do my own will but the will of him who sent me."
- John 15:10 (ESV): "If you keep my commandments, you will abide in my love, just as I have kept my Father's commandments and abide in his love."

Clearly, Jesus attributed His authority and power to submitting to His Father. He knew that His stewardship had unprecedented authority and power to fulfill a specific purpose, but not for his own ego or to appease those who were listening. His task was to bring the whole family of God together.

Here is the irony of it all: David came to the cave much earlier than the others. Everything he had acquired had been taken away. His heroic reputation was no longer intact; he was broke, broken, and in serious danger. After losing his momentum, this was the result of his first two visitations from God:

- He discovered that God was inside that cave. In fact, God had never left him. Through repentance and submission, God had been restored to His rightful position as the head, or the "first," in David's life.
- His family had come to join him. Actually, it was David's family who had restored his self-confidence and renewed his perspective about what was worth fighting for.

Perhaps clarity of purpose was one of the truths the men of Adullam had learned. They had finally discovered whom God made them to be, what He had given them, and why He had given it to them. It's possible that helping these broken, confused, disconnected, and sedated men to see a fresh perspective was God's true purpose for them. In fact, the starting point for this uncommon clarity was their wives and families.

Many men waste an exorbitant amount of time, focus, and energy trying to find a cause. They need something to get them up in the morning and a reason to be more, have more, and achieve more. My prayer is that every man will begin to see this liberating, empowering truth: what you've been looking for all along has been right there under your nose. If you'll accept that fight, the rewards are enormous!

The Fight of Your Life

In 2 Peter 1:5-7, we are admonished to add to our faith virtue. The Greek word for virtue is *arete*, meaning excellence in strength or "masculine excellence."

In the context of 2 Peter, most translators lean toward moral strength. The Greeks, however, typically used this word in the context of "muscular" or "masculine" faith. In the battle between Persia and Greece in the fifth century, the Persians tried for 50 years to defeat the Greeks and could not. The Persians drove their enslaved men into battle with whips and prods, trying their best to motivate them through shame and fear.

However, the Greek Spartans fought as free men. They fought for their families and their land. To them, the word *arete* was about adding focused strength to their battle. Focusing on their families and their land gave specificity to their faith that produced a superior strength.

The way to elevate your posture as a man and add to your faith in God is gaining clarity concerning your family and home. That is the source of masculine strength and excellence.

Never underestimate the power of doing the right thing. God will make it count for something great.

Your family is worth fighting for, not just because they're a good thing, but because they're a God-thing! Your adversary, the devil, has a battle plan, and your family becomes the spoils of his warfare.

When you fight for your family, you're fighting for future generations. The totality of the power and authority God has enabled you to possess is not for some random, rogue purpose. It's for you to till your garden, lead your home, and empower your family to experience God's best for them.

Too many men strategize about how to conquer the world when they're not even fruitful or productive in their own homes. My brother, this is your garden. It is your starting point. It is the place where the credibility of all you think you are is either affirmed or diminished.

There's nothing more impressive or attractive than a man who loves, honors, and respects his queen, admires and protects his kids, and leads each of them into their God-given destiny.

Can this be exhausting? Sure. Can it feel at times that you're giving more than you're receiving? Sure. But this is the fight we men must be willing and ready to engage in. It's what we were created to do. When you lead your family in the ways of God, He will reward and replenish you.

You don't find a great marriage. You don't find a fabulous family. You don't find the ideal home or the perfect career. *You build one.* That's what God did! He created humanity so He could build a family. And for a while, everything seemed to be going downhill. His family took advantage of Him, drifted away from Him, and even attempted to replace Him. But a family is worth fighting for — and fight He did! God sacrificed Jesus to redeem His family. Your faith in Christ will restore you to His glorious family!

In the book of Nehemiah, there's a powerful analogy that shows the reality of this fight. After 70 years of captivity in Babylon, King Cyrus finally gave the children of Israel permission to return to their land and rebuild their temple. He even provided the finances to rebuild it. While many adversaries conspired against them on a daily basis, they kept working. It took 20 years to complete the temple, but they finally finished it!

Then they realized that the temple would be in jeopardy without a wall around it for protection. The wall would defend them from their enemies and protect their community and house of worship. Every man was assigned to build a particular section of the wall. It just so happened that they were building their homes into the structure of the wall. In other words, a solid wall consisted of solid homes. Each man's home and the space surrounding his home were the territory he was assigned to build. Essentially, each man built his house and joined with other men doing the same to form a wall, which in turn would fortify the temple.

In Nehemiah 4, something incredible happened. Israel's enemies heard about this wall being built; they strategized to come against them and destroy them. But when Israel's leaders learned about their plan, they said,

> So I stationed people behind the lowest sections of the wall, at the vulnerable areas. I stationed them by families with their swords, spears, and bows. After I made an inspection, I stood up and said to the nobles, the officials, and the rest of the people, "Don't be afraid of them. Remember the great and awe-inspiring Lord, and fight for your countrymen, your sons and daughters, your wives and homes … Whenever you hear the sound of the trumpet, rally to us there. Our God will fight for us." (Neh. 4:13-14, 20 CSB)

As they built the wall, every man held a trowel in one hand and a sword in the other. It only took 52 days to complete it. Imagine that! It took 20 years to rebuild the temple, but only 52 days to build a wall of protection for their families.

Every man was building and fighting, not for just a wall, but for his family! When men rise up and fight for their families, something supernatural occurs! They feel strength they did not know was available. With all their hearts, these men believed that *if you fight for your family, God will fight for you!*

A Fight That Is Bigger Than You

When a man is healed and set free, he understands that he's fighting for more than just that moment. When you're fully aligned with God, He will elevate you to a fantastic place. Since our transcendent God operates outside of time, space, and geography, He does not speak or act for just that moment. He's forever operating with eternity in mind. His mighty presence that resides and operates in us changes the game!

Since God exists outside of space and time, He sees the end from the beginning. When He gives you something, it's in seed form. That seed incorporates the history, experience, and equity of days gone by, as well as an unlimited potential for the future—in just one word. For this present dimension, that ideal is the word "legacy."

Since your life's agenda did not begin with you, you should remember that it won't end with you either. You can't get lost in the pursuit of money and toys. God has an equity in you. It's His story traveling through you. He expects it to be manifested in your family and then continue for generations to come. This is what the stewardship of legacy is all about.

Something is traveling through you that's not just for you. It's the story of God and the equity of the past that has made you a steward to reach generations that will come after you!

Think of this: God takes a seed, a word, or a promise that has a multi-generational life span of at least 120-140 years. However, He deposits it into the life of someone who may only live to be 70-75 years old. That means that what many of us are carrying is not really even for us and may not come to completion in our lifetime. The great patriarchs and matriarchs of scripture seemed to know this well, and it was fine with them. After listing many of their names in Hebrews 11:13 (NIV), the scripture says, "All these people were still living by faith when they died. They did not receive the things promised; they only saw them and welcomed them from a distance, admitting that they were foreigners and strangers on earth."

But they were okay with that because even the mere pursuit of God's purpose produced a life that was unforgettable.

If your life is not spent on something that will live longer than you, you will have wasted your time.
—Jim Miller

Think of the many great visitations from God that have been short-lived. The awakening God planned to unfold over three generations was poured out upon a generation of consumers rather than stewards.

The truth is that God's promises are not usually front-loaded. They are designed to pack the greatest punch toward the end, which could be generations down the road. Many of His blessings are still in the process of being developed. I am convinced that most of us have yet to experience God's best for us. We've felt the jab and thought it was the knockout punch!

After God had promised Abraham that his descendants would be as numerous as the stars in the sky and the sand by the seashore, he chose to become a living example for future generations to follow. Notice how his life was a steady progression of God's promises:

- Abraham spent his life building altars and accumulating wealth.
- His son Isaac spent his life digging wells.
- Isaac's son Jacob spent his life raising a family of twelve sons.
- Jacob/Israel's twelve sons birthed a nation.

As God's mighty man, He has entrusted you to fight for a family who will become the recipients of God's power working through them. My brother, what you have been given is so magnificent that it will take at least three generations for it to come to pass. The fight is much bigger than you!

In Deuteronomy 6, God spoke to the nation of Israel that His laws, commandments, and promises must extend to the following generations. In fact, He specifically said:

> That you may fear the Lord your God, to keep all His statutes and His commandments which I command you, you and your son and your grandson, all the days of your life, and that your days may be prolonged. (Deut. 6:2, NKJV)

In the remainder of chapter 6, He said,

> And these words which I command you today shall be in your heart. You shall teach them diligently to your children, and shall talk of them when you sit in your house, when you walk by the way, when you lie down, and when you rise up. You shall bind them as a sign on your hand, and they shall be as frontlets between your eyes. You shall write them on the doorposts of your house and on your gates. (Deut. 6:6-9 NKJV)

After reading this chapter, we can only conclude that God's expectations were both intentional and obsessive. That's how the fight must be for you!

You must determine that you are going to be obsessed with fighting for your family and their God-given purpose and destiny. You must be both intentional and obsessive because you have limits when it comes to your time, energy, and focus capacity. You cannot give yourself to all things at all times. You have to carefully monitor and measure the things you invest your life in.

Far too many men who honestly love and care for their families give too much of themselves to other pursuits, activities, and goals. Then, when it comes to the thing God expects them to treat with the highest priority, they just don't have anything left to give. They'll say things like, "My wife is just too demanding." Or, "My family just pulls so much out of me." What may be happening is that your wife and kids might be acting out of their own deficiency —a deficiency you may have helped to create. One that is the fruit of their head and spiritual covering not investing what he should have in them.

King David spent most of his reign preparing materials, money, and provision for his son, Solomon, to build a new temple. This father was fighting for future generations to fulfill their purpose on the earth. Could this shift have occurred while he was in the cave?

Like these great fighters for Israel, our churches and communities desperately need men who will fight for their homes and families. When we fight to build a strong family, we're also making our churches, communities, and nations stronger.

What the Fight Looks Like

A man who is committed to fighting for his family and home can easily be recognized.

He prays, works, and provides for the needs of his family before his own. Nothing is more pitiful than seeing kids wearing worn-out shoes while dad has the latest watch, phone, or toys.

He leads by example. As stated earlier, a man does not reproduce what he wishes or hopes for. He reproduces who and what he is. Show your family what submission to God looks like. Show them what prayer, fasting, and worship look like. Live as if the only way they'll ever see Jesus is through your example. If you do, they'll begin their own relationship with Christ soon enough.

Most families spell love t-i-m-e. The best way to communicate the sincerity of your new resolve is by spending quality time with your family. A school play, baseball games, and family games around a kitchen table are so important. A weekly date night with your wife is crucial. Refuse to address your personal challenges or "vent" your frustrations. Once a week, take the time to thoroughly enjoy each other.

The truth is that everything that you schedule will get done. I have worked with a lot of executives and professional athletes who are notorious for scheduling conference calls, product roll-out dates, business meetings, and to-do lists. But when I ask them to show me their schedule for quality time with their kids and a weekly "date night" with their wife, they look at me like a deer staring in the headlights of an approaching car. It's usually not on their schedule. Most say that those events should be spontaneous and organic. Really? As opposed to it not happening at all? If it is not scheduled, it usually won't be remembered. *Everything* in life that matters should be scheduled. At some point, it may become automatic, but most men are not there yet. Forming a habit of scheduling these sacred things will show your household how much it really matters and how intentional it is for you.

Pay attention. You should know what is lurking around in your home, both spiritually and physically. Numerous unseen forces are fighting to lead your family away from God and His purposes. You should keep your finger on the pulse of every member of your family. Not by dominant micro-managing or smothering, but by praying for awareness and discernment—and by simply walking around with your eyes open!

Be an "edifier." The word edification (*oikodome*), which is used 20 times in the New Testament, literally means "the building of a house." A man fighting for his family is not just maintaining an aggressive posture outside the home against all adversaries. He is also digging deep and calling out the best in every member of his family. The rest of the world—friends, bullies, school, peers, etc. —will take care of the criticism and negativity. What you need to do is speak life over your family with a loud voice—even if it seems that you're speaking into dead things. A mighty man must develop the ability to edify.

David and his men found a renewed sense of purpose in the cave of Adullam to fight for their families. Fight for future generations. Fight for your family to have a place to worship God and live in His abundant blessing and favor. When these men emerged from the cave, they were ready. They were the mighty!

Small-Group Discussion Points

- *Gather your family together and ask them to forgive you if they have ever felt that you were not fighting for them.* Your thoughts on this subject are irrelevant. Perception is greater than reality. So, don't be defensive or argumentative. Just tell them you're going to do better and then *do it*!
- *Become the spiritual leader in your family by guiding conversations and activities toward the purposes of God.* It may seem a bit awkward at first to jump in with a full-blown family altar. But don't sweat it. Try to guide your

family through a daily, real-life experience from God's perspective. Help them talk their way through challenges they may be facing.

- *Thank God every day for trusting you to be the steward for your family.* He allowed you to have a family because He knew you could not only handle it but would be an excellent leader.
- Ask God to change your whole perspective and thought process from consumption to stewardship.
- *Take an inventory of your family's vocabulary.* Change what is negative, critical, and pessimistic to words that will edify and build each other. Talk with your wife and children about the many good things that are happening in your family.

9

Don't Forget You!

In response to being asked about the greatest commandment, Jesus answered, "You shall love the Lord your God with all your heart, with all your soul, and with all your mind. This is the first and great commandment. And the second is like it: You shall love your neighbor as yourself" (Matt. 22:37-39 KJV).

I am not contradicting a mighty man's priorities from an earlier chapter. As Jesus said, God must be first, or you're finished! And you absolutely must fight sacrificially for your family. But to do these things well, you must become the very best version of yourself.

To truly "love your neighbor as yourself," your love for God, family, friends, and community will be enhanced or diminished according to the degree you love yourself. When you have a healthy love and respect for yourself, it will spill over to other parts of your life. You cannot effectively reign in your world unless you build yourself up!

I've counseled godly men who really cared about their families and had a strong desire to treat them well. But they may die 15-20 years too soon because they're so unhealthy and/or obese from failing to care for themselves. Their investment in building themselves up was minimal. Your family, church, and community want you to be the best version of yourself you can possibly be. They want you to train, study, learn, and grow so you can lead them into new adventures and experiences.

We have talked about putting God first and dwelling in the secret place of His presence. Now I want to challenge you in a few other areas of life. A mighty man must diligently expose himself to patterns and habits that are more constructive. Specifically, if you're chasing after God like a mad man, you must diligently invest in these areas.

Grow Your Intellect

A man who wants to be at the top where he belongs must be intellectually sound and admirable. I'm not talking about being a Harvard graduate or a member of the Mensa Society. I'm talking about reading, studying, and expanding your knowledge in areas that will further empower you to lead your family after the order of David's cave men.

God created you with intellect and the ability to reason, comprehend, and learn. King Solomon, the wisest man who ever lived (next to Jesus), said: "Wisdom is the most valuable commodity, so buy it! Revelation knowledge is what you need, so invest in it!" (Prov. 4:7, TPT).

The Bible tells us that even Jesus, the Son of God, who had the fullness of the Spirit from His mother's womb, continued to grow in wisdom and understanding. His wisdom was already ahead of the curve, far beyond His years. At the age of 12, the Jewish teachers and scholars were amazed at His understanding. But He kept growing.

In Luke 2:52 (NIV), we are told, "And Jesus grew in wisdom and stature, and in favor with God and man." For 30 years, He learned, studied, and increased His capacity to grow and understand.

Study the art of spiritual warfare. Know your enemy. Study strategies that build great families. Learn about current trends and activities that appeal to your children. Read literature about financial management and budgeting. Learn the ABCs of basic investments so you can build an inheritance for your family. It's not good for a man to know less about most things than everyone else in his household. Again, I'm not talking about your IQ rating. The Holy Spirit within you is the ultimate teacher of truth. Jesus promised that the Holy Spirit would guide you from within. Best of all, scripture declares that God will freely give wisdom to those who ask Him.

Paul instructed his spiritual son, Timothy, "Study to shew thyself approved unto God, a workman that needeth not to be ashamed, rightly dividing the word of truth. But shun profane and vain babblings: for they will increase unto more ungodliness" (2 Tim. 2:15-16 KJV).

I talk to way too many older men who have the same conversations, jokes, ideals, patterns, and opinions that they did when they were 18. Nothing has changed. They reached adulthood by age, then stopped growing.

Remember to have conversations with mentors and fathers about subjects that are deeper than sports or Netflix specials. You won't be permitted to reign just because you have been anointed to do so. You must qualify yourself to walk in that capacity of rule.

A mighty man must also enlarge his understanding to fulfill a higher position when it's time for God to promote him. What if your boss said, "Beginning next week, we're promoting you to the regional manager of our company," and you knew hardly anything about that position?

The first thing you would say is, "Yes!" That's what a mighty man would do—and then figure it out. You would accept the promotion and then take a deep dive into learning and preparing yourself for this new role.

That's exactly what a mighty man, who wants to rule and reign with Christ, would do. If God has called and anointed you to be a leader in your particular world, maximize your readiness.

A man will be the same five years from now as he is today, except for the people he meets and the books he reads.
—Charlie "Tremendous" Jones

If you fail to increase your cognitive capacity, you'll be outmatched. Then you'll find yourself falling back on this ineffective and outdated posture: "Just do what I say because I'm your dad." Or, "Because I'm the man of this house." That won't work any longer.

While Jesus spoke sharply and directly with argumentative religious people, most of His time was spent teaching truth to the ordinary man by painting word pictures with analogies and parables. Since He was in the business of persuading people, His focus was not on winning an argument but helping them understand the better way He was teaching them.

Life is moving at a rapid pace; technology is expanding faster than we can keep up. Trends pop up overnight, and cultural dynamics are changing with the wind. You must not waste your time digesting more of the same old stuff you've talked about for years. Read, study, challenge your-self, and constantly learn. That's what you were born to do!

Master Your Emotions

Proverbs 16:32 (KJV) says, "He that is slow to anger is better than the mighty; and he that ruleth his spirit than he that taketh a city."

If there's one thing that will sabotage a man's success quicker than anything else, it's to have unchecked emotions. Dale Carnegie said, "When dealing with people, remember you are not dealing with creatures of logic, but with creatures of emotion." In a world that runs on feelings and emotions, it's so important to maintain a superior posture in those inner-personal relationships.

Of course, it's important for a man to feel and be aware of his emotions. But it's not okay for your emotions to take the lead. Happiness, sadness, fear, anger, surprise, and disgust are some basic areas of emotion that we experience. And you cannot (nor should you want) to divorce yourself from those feelings. Emotional mastery is not the practice of suppressing emotions; rather, it is learning how to effectively manage them. A mighty man must excel in emotional intelligence.

God had some pretty stringent requirements for priests when they had to manage their emotions in times of mourning or crisis.

- The priests who ministered in the outer courts were allowed to mourn for seven days. Then they had to dry their tears, wash their faces, and continue to function in their calling.
- The priests who ministered in the inner court were allowed to mourn for three days, then had to get back to work.
- The priest who entered the Holiest Place was only allowed one day for mourning.
- An even more extreme requirement was given to a national prophet. In Ezekiel 24, God told Ezekiel that his wife would pass away before the morning. But God would not permit him to participate in any types of customary mourning. He was told in advance so that he could be prepared to stand before the people.

That may seem a bit insensitive, but here is the two-fold principle: the higher you go and the more people look to you for leadership, the more important it is to control your emotions. Likewise, the more effective you are in managing your emotions, the higher in life you will go.

You are far more capable of controlling your emotions than you may think. How many times have you answered the phone in the middle of a heated and quickly escalating conversation, took a deep breath, cleared your throat, and answered in your normal voice? Probably, lots of times. Because you wanted to save face, save your job, or make an impression on someone, you found the strength to override your emotions. A mighty man realizes that emotional intelligence matters and it's *always* important!

Many marriages have been irretrievably damaged, business opportunities sabotaged, relationships destroyed, and opportunities squandered, not because of some measure of incompetence, but because somebody didn't control their emotions and reacted in a way that was counterproductive to success. Words were spoken out of ramped up emotions, decisions were made when feelings trumped reason and logic, and good patterns were broken because of a fleeting emotion that wasn't kept in check. Here are a few comparisons:

Mighty Man	*Average Man*
Emotional management	Emotional suppression
Strategic/calculated response	Knee-jerk reactions
Feelings kept in perspective	Runs with feelings
Controls his volume	Given to outbursts
Controls his physiology	Grits teeth, clenches fists
Gathers data for decisions	Reacts to partial data
Effectively analyzes self	Always justifies self
Builds relationships	Sabotages relationships

The list could go on and on, but hopefully you get the picture. Emotional mastery is easier for some than others, but it can be achieved by all. Some of us have witnessed great coping skills and conflict resolution techniques as we were growing up, but others have not. Some of us run hot, while others are more subdued. Some of us are easily excitable, and some are not.

I fully believe there is a great difference between nature and nurture. Nature genetically transfers things to us. By nature, I am 5 ft. 11 in. tall, and I have a thick and dense bone structure. My eyes are blue, and my hair is light brown. These are part of my nature. However, the explosive nature of unchecked emotions largely comes through nurturing. Coping skills, vocabulary, mannerisms, acceptable childhood behavior, conversational models, standards of respect, and honor are just a few of the behaviors we absorb simply by being exposed to them as children. These same dynamics are also responsible for forming our emotional intelligence as adults. The good news is that anything we learned by nurture can just as easily be re-learned.

I love the following image that is used by top behavioral experts in our country. It's my favorite visual to guide the simplicity and efficiency of emotional management.

It is important to know that once you have prayed, read the Word, and worshiped, there are still a number of effective coping mechanisms that will contribute to mastering your emotions. The synergy of language, physiology, and focus can have a powerful impact in this process.

Physiology

The difference between talking with clenched fists and gritted teeth and talking with normal posture is quite substantial. Pay attention to your physical posture when you're feeling strong emotions. They always mean something. You can't allow the fact that real emotions are being experienced to mean that they can be in charge.

Specific neurological functions within the brain are responsible for a particular response when we perceive that someone or something is threatening us or trying to disrupt our wellbeing. An elevated heart rate, tense muscles, elevated blood pressure, increased breathing, and a burst of energy may last for several minutes. We may encounter these feelings because our brains are wired to act before considering the consequences of our actions. Intentional physiology becomes quite critical while managing the effects of these natural body functions. The more you learn to regulate these factors, the greater chance you will have to make good judgments and decisions.

Every emotion has a corresponding physical expression that's either defensive or pro-active. Open your fists and your teeth, and you will relieve tension. Breathe slower and deeper and walk around a bit, and you will clear your thoughts and reset your mood. Stand up straight, and you will feel more confident. Do whatever you have to do to regulate the effects in your body and limit their role in choosing what you say and do.

Focus

Whatever you focus on will capture your energy. When you focus on things that are wrong—what you don't have, who's holding you back, or a myriad of other negative thoughts—your energy will drain right out of you. Where you direct your focus will determine your intentions. Every one of your internal systems will follow your intentions.

I love what Proverbs 4:25 (NIV) says: "Let your eyes look straight ahead; fix your gaze directly before you." This is one way to control the internal narrative that's resounding in your head. We all have these ongoing conversations and narratives in our thoughts. These are some of the most important conversations you'll ever have because, at the end of the day, you will either convince yourself of your greatness or talk yourself out of it.

> Finally, brothers and sisters, whatever is true, whatever is noble, whatever is right, whatever is pure, whatever is lovely, whatever is admirable—if anything is excellent or praiseworthy— think about such things. (Phil. 4:8 NIV)

If you focus on how things once were, you'll miss out on how things can be. If you focus on lack, scarcity, revenge, regret, etc., you'll get more of the same. But you are becoming a mighty man. You are not gazing at what everyone else is doing. You are looking at the things no one else can see at the moment. And in time, you'll have what few others have!

Language

For centuries, the experts have operated on the assumption that language was relegated to being expressive or reflective of our emotions. Only in recent decades has the psychological community recognized that the power of language can assist in managing our emotions rather than describing them after the fact. In other words, our language has the power to control an emotion than simply describe one.

Our words have the power to create perception and give new meaning to an emotion, or even reshape its nature. Greatly simplified, you may not be able to stop elevated breathing, heart rate, blood pressure, muscle tension, or a burst of energy, but your language can determine what it all means and how you will respond to it. It is a powerful tool to take control of that internal commentator that just never shuts up!

Every man needs to build his vocabulary with words that do not incite negative responses. But the middle of a heated conversation is not the ideal time to do this. A mighty man should discipline his vocabulary in his quiet and reflective times, then stick with it at all times and in all circumstances. Someone once said, "Be sure to taste your own words before you spit them out."

Vocabulary is mastering word-building,
as well as word-using.
—David Crystal

Language patterns and phrases are easier to correct than you might think. It just takes some analysis and commitment to make the changes. Scott Adams said, "Your inability to see other possibilities and your lack of vocabulary are the limitations of your own brain, not the universe!"

Since we know that to change your life you must change your mind, that thoughts are the results of words, and that words create thoughts, here's a better way to make the above statement: "If you want to change your life, change your vocabulary." And, if you want to change other people's lives, change your vocabulary in ways that edify others and cause them to gravitate toward success.

Ask yourself these questions: "Are there specific words that I often use that constantly summon negative emotions in me? What words do I use that reinforce limitations? What do I regularly say that supports insecurity and a negative complex?"

Write these words down and then cross them off only when every single one has been replaced with a word that incites vision, faith, hope, clarity, and confidence.

In short, your emotions are the body's reaction to the activity of your mind. Take control of your mind and you will gain control of your emotions.

Build Your Temple

This may be the shortest of the three points in this chapter, but it is no less critical. Volumes of books have been written about physical health and fitness, including dieting programs, Keto lifestyles, CrossFit gyms, beach bodies, and more. The list is endless.

There's never a shortage of content for a man who's looking for fitness or dietary advice. My intention is not to dive into any of that. You can follow that on your own. I simply want you to get off the couch and get this done! You don't have to aspire to be a professional bodybuilder or a world-class iron-man. But it *is* time for all of us to respect the temple God has given us.

> Do you not know that you are the temple of God and that the Spirit of God dwells in you? If anyone defiles the temple of God, God will destroy him. For the temple of God is holy, which temple you are. (1 Cor. 3:16-17 NKJV)

I realize that this verse refers to the abiding presence of the Holy Spirit within us. But the admonition should not end there. I acknowledge that a gym membership may not be your thing; intense training regimens may intimidate you. I get it. But I want you to get motivated to stop making excuses and start making changes. A mighty man needs stamina. He needs energy and a clear head. He needs to be healthy enough to stick around for the long haul.

One of the most important abilities a man can possess is to influence others. As a leader, you should continually engage in persuading people—your family, friends, co-workers, and associates—to follow every aspect of your life. The entirety of your life is like a billboard that persuades people to follow the path you have chosen to pursue.

Poor health standards, sloppy eating habits, no concern for fitness, and neglecting your physical body reveals a serious lack of discipline. People won't follow leaders who are undisciplined. If you're 80 years old, you might get a pass for not being able to walk a lap with your grandkids, but when you're 45 or 50, not so much. My intention is not to shame or ridicule anyone for health issues beyond their control. But a mighty man should continually pay attention to his physical stamina and condition.

This is not a commitment to become a world-class athlete; it's just following these simple habits: exercise every day, eat clean and healthy food, drink lots of water, get plenty of sleep, dress like you're going somewhere, take some pride in your appearance, remove the sugar and processed food from your house, etc. You get the point! Your family, church, and community need you to be around long enough to put up a good fight for them!

Small-Group Discussion Points

- *Commit to reading more:* Set some goals for yourself, like one book every week or month. Choose books that will further empower and equip you as a mighty man, not just entertain you.
- *Plan in-depth, weekly conversations with mentors:* Be diligent about expanding your capacity for wisdom and understanding.
- *Begin writing a plan to master your emotions:* Include ways to incorporate the principles in this chapter for language, physiology, and focus.
- *Start a daily exercise program* **today***:* Even if it's just a few laps around the block every day, start now. You don't want to be a slave to everyone's opinion about your appearance, but you do want to influence people to follow Jesus. And you want to be around for a while to do it! Drink more water and get better sleep. No excuses. You have been anointed to do better and be better.

10

Get Back in the Game

To get back on top and "have it all," being *all in*
must characterize you! You will have to surrender everything you are and all that you have to your Maker. When it
comes to God's purpose for your life, any reservation will
be reflected in other areas of your life. You can't possibly
love God *with reservation* and fully love your wife, family,
and others. It's just not possible!

To be a Mighty Man, you will have to love without reservation, give without hesitation, fight with conviction, and
lead with inspiration. This is a principle of the mighty:

If you're going to be a bear, be a grizzly!
Anything else is just a bear!

If you're going to do something, do it big, do it right,
do it first-class, and go all out, or don't even get out of bed.
I love what the great Fred Astaire said: "Do it Big, do it
right, and do it with style." Nothing will have a profound
domino effect in your life like applying this attitude to your
relationship with God. When you're all in and completely
invested in Him, there's an incredible force that touches

everything in life that matters to God and demands that it multiply and prosper.

Somebody once said, "Live every day like it was your last, every night like it was your first, and every moment like it was God's last gift to you." That's all in with some grandiose bravado thrown in. I love it!

You can't outwit fate by trying to stand on the sidelines and place little side bets about the outcome of life. Either you wade in and risk everything to play the game, or you don't play at all. And if you don't play, you can't win.
—Judith McNaught

In Matthew 13:44 (NKJV), Jesus said: "The kingdom of heaven is like a treasure hidden in a field, which a man found and hid; and for joy over it he goes and sells all that he has and buys the field." That's what you call all in. Give everything you have to get the treasure.

Matthew 19:16-22 (NKJV) tells the story of a young man who asked Jesus what he needed to do to inherit eternal life. Without question, Jesus' response was an admonition for an "all in" attitude.

He gave the young man a list of things he should do (before the cross, I might add). After Jesus mentioned some basic commandments, the young man replied, "Teacher, all of these things I have kept from my youth." Then Jesus challenged him with this statement: "One thing you lack: Go your way, sell whatever you have and give to the poor."

The young man went home sorrowful because he was not ready for that degree of all in.

Jesus was not implying that you will have to be broke to please God. But you *must* be willing to give up whatever is necessary to gain the Kingdom of God and His purpose for your life.

Here is the bottom line: a partial commitment, or even a delayed commitment, is not really a commitment at all. God's expectation of you as a warrior and mighty man is to throw yourself at His feet with reckless abandon and go for the whole thing—with everything you have got. *All in!*

If you're going to be thinking anything,
you might as well think big.
—Donald Trump

Come on, mighty man; you've got this. How could it work any other way? Let yourself dream a little. What would life be like if your walk with God was totally dialed in, you were knocking it out of the park as a husband and a father, you were healthy and in good shape, your income had sky-rocketed, and *everything* in your life was in the rhythm of success and greatness? You will never know—until you give it your *all!*

If you have been waiting on God, let me settle that for you: you have simply been wasting time. No, you're not waiting on God; He's been waiting on you! Sometimes people pray for a miracle or dramatic change when they're really asking God to do the things they don't have the courage to do for themselves.

---

*Sometimes your passion must go up in flames
before you can go down in history.*
—Curtis Tyrone Jones

Courage is not the absence of fear, apprehension, or even a bit of doubt. It's taking action in spite of it! In my years as a professional cage fighter, I was often interviewed about my role in the sport, and it would go something like this:

> *Interviewer:* "Are you ever scared right before a fight?"
>
> *Me:* "If you mean jumping out of the cage and running out of the arena, then, *no!* But if you mean sweaty palms, butterflies in my stomach, and that little inner voice saying, 'You can still get out of this,' then *yes!*"
>
> *Interviewer:* "Then what did you do or how did you handle that?"
>
> *Me:* "You fight scared! It does not take long before a punch is thrown, a kick executed, or a take-down attempted, and suddenly all of that goes away."

This has been a guiding principle all of my life. Sometimes you have to acknowledge your feelings, identify your fears and anxiety, and then *get up and do it anyway!*

Maybe you have already tried that or had some energetic resolutions in times past. Perhaps you have watched people you admire and care about try and fail. Maybe that inner voice was screaming at you: "What if you try and everyone sees you fail? What will other people think about you?"

Whatever the source of your fear, just know it's not credible. Who cares if you try and fail? What if you fall and people laugh at you? What does everyone else's opinion matter anyway? The world is kind toward people who keep on trying. But they are not very keen on those who try, fail, and then stop trying.

Let's not sugarcoat this. Whatever knocked you out of the game or kept you from joining won't go away without a fight. Old habits die hard. Old friends and associations are sure to show up at the worst possible moment. You'll have plenty of reasons to go back to the way things were, but don't do it! There's nothing for you back there.

Your game of life has not ended, whether you have been participating in it or not. The battle goes on. It's time to get off the sidelines. You can't win any victories there or make any worthwhile contributions. All you can do is be a spectator.

Remember the story of the disciples crossing the sea when a terrible storm threatened their lives? In the middle of the storm, Jesus came walking on the water and invited Peter to come. Was he terrified? Probably. Anxious? No doubt. Full of faith and expectation? Most likely not.

Don't imitate the disciples who were sitting in the boat, waiting for Peter to make a fool of himself. *He got out of the boat anyway!* When the power of God came upon Peter, he began walking on the water toward Jesus. Yes, about halfway there he looked around at the intimidating limitations of the raging sea and started sinking, but Jesus took his hand, and they walked back to the boat together *on the water*! Back to the boat filled with spectators!

No one could tell that story of walking on the water like Peter. The other disciples stayed with the familiar and where they were most comfortable. Little did they know that the comfortable and familiar was in serious trouble! Peter was the first to discover that he was safer in the boisterous waves because Jesus was there!

The old you, the old life, and your old ways may seem more familiar and comfortable, but they're not! If you stay there, you'll perish. Leave it behind. The safest and best place is *on the water*, surrounded by crashing waves, unfamiliar territory, and danger *with Jesus*! Get back in the game!

Small-Group Discussion Points to Help You Get Back in the Game

- *Change the conversation going on within you.*
  Denial, ignorance, and arrogance are not the way to go. There's no need to downplay real adversity. Telling yourself, "I'm the greatest! Nobody can stop me!" is pointless, as is saying, "What if I fail?" What if you do fail? There's never been a champion or anyone who has become memorable who *didn't* fail. It's all part of the game. A better question is this: *"What if I win?"* The internal conversation of a mighty man would more than likely go like this: "This is not going to be easy. I have got some real adversaries out there. Everybody does not want me to succeed. Not

everybody will appreciate what I'm doing. People who should be supporting me are hoping I will fail. I'm going to have to learn new things. There will be moments when I will wonder if I can do this. But what if I succeed?! What if I can totally change my family's future? My family, my church, and my community are hoping I will go all in on this. So, if I fall, I will just get up and keep trying. If I embarrass myself, I will try it again. But, if I succeed, it will change the trajectory of my entire legacy. Since there's only one way to find out, here I go!"

- *Stop making excuses; eliminate them from both your inward and outward conversations.* No one cares about your excuses. Your family and friends don't believe the excuses, and your enemies are not listening. So why and how you got there is not important now. Benjamin Franklin said, "He that is good at making excuses is seldom good for anything else." Your transformation into a mighty man is a team sport. People are praying for you that you don't even know. You have new mentors/fathers and a new brotherhood of like-minded cave men who are pursuing exactly what you're pursuing.

- *Know you're not alone.* Most importantly, God is for you and will never be against you. Always look up! My good friend, Les Brown, said, "If you fall down, pray that you fall flat on your back; cuz if you can look up, you can get up!" Don't focus on the immediate circumstances before you. Look at it from a higher perspective. From God's vantage point, things look totally different than what's right in front of you. And His vantage point is always the most accurate!

- *Remember the long-term goal.* The story of your life is an accumulation of many chapters. Some people will try to judge you according to the particular chapter they happen to see. Dismiss their negative criticism. One chapter does not tell the whole story. Some chapters will be great and inspiring, while others will be a preview of things to come. Some chapters will convince your readers of the outcome, while others will make them wonder if you're going to make it. Just remember, one chapter does not tell the whole story. This is the end of your story: God trusts you. As the author and finisher of your life's story, He is for you. He has already determined that you will win *if you don't quit.*

- *Remember who and what you're fighting for.* Remind yourself daily that God trusts you enough to become a steward of something that's bigger than you. Treasure your family and believe in the destiny God has for them. When you fight for His cause, the rewards are staggering!

David's men followed his lead. They gave up their pain and disappointments and returned to God with their whole hearts. They were healed and free from the problems that had driven them to the cave. They were refreshed and renewed. Their purpose was defined with greater clarity: fight for your family so that your community and nation will become stronger.

When they emerged, they were focused, fierce, determined, and infused with the power of God. No longer were they broken, defeated, and discouraged men. Everything had changed. They had found a cave and were now connected to a leader. That's how they became the mighty!

Now it's your turn, mighty man of God. Get ready and *go!*